FOODGASM

PLANT-BASED: VOLUME ONE

DON'T FAKE IT.
96 RECIPES SO GOOD NO ONE WILL BELIEVE THEY'RE PLANT-BASED

FEATURING JESSICA KLEIN

FOOD · GASM

n. Intense, sensual excitement inspired by delicious food.

Eating should be one of the most sensual, pleasurable experiences in life. That's why we created Foodgasm, a collection of books featuring some of today's top culinary stars who share their secrets for cooking simple, deeply satisfying meals anyone can learn to make—meals so good you'll never have to fake it again.

We're making food sexy again, one bite at a time.

978-1-7358218-3-2

Foodgasm® is a registered trademark of Foodgasm, LLC. All rights reserved.

For my children, may you always know how much you are loved.
You are magic.

As humans, we need three things to survive: food, sex and shelter. To move from surviving to thriving you have to add in pleasure. That's where Foodgasm comes in. Food is literally about nourishing our bodies. Food helps us relax, connect, and come together with the people we care about the most. Cooking should not be stressful. I created these recipes because I love great tasting food.

But, let's be honest, I have a lot on my plate.

I am a mom to three boys, a homemaker, and I have a career. By the time dinner comes around, I don't want to think about it. When I wake in the morning I have so many things to do, and stressing over making sure my kids get plenty of nutrients is not one of them. They need to grow their bodies and balance their crazy #boymom. They love a good Starbucks vanilla bean Frappuccino — coconut milk, double blended, no whip — but that's not an ideal breakfast.

We have people pop by all. the. time. I need easy snacks to put out that look like I give a f*ck — because I do, however there are higher things on my priority list than standing in a kitchen for hours for snacks, or an impromptu dinner. Which is funny, because I often spend hours in the kitchen all day — I want to be in there because I choose to be, not feel obligated. I want good food. I want time with my kids. I want to rock my career.

I want time for myself. I want it all, and I want it all for you. I hope it helps you live your best life, fuel your body, and give you the time to do what you need and want while filling your belly with yummy foodgasms that won't expand your waistline.

Jessica

TABLE OF CONTENTS

BREAKFAST

ACAI BOWL

GRANOLA

½ cup walnuts

½ cup almonds

¼ cup sunflower seeds

¼ cup pumpkin seeds

¼ cup dates

2 tablespoons flaxseeds

1 tablespoon coconut oil

½ teaspoon vanilla

ACAI MIX

4 packages frozen acai

½ cup coconut oil

1 banana (*frozen best if eating right away*)

1 cup blueberries (*frozen or fresh*)

2 tablespoons sweetener of choice (*maple syrup to monk fruit - it's all good*)

¼ cup cacao powder

2 tablespoons maca

1 pinch sea salt

OPTIONAL GARNISH

fresh cut fruit

coconut flakes

dried fruit

fresh herbs

chocolate sauce

SERVES: 4
TOTAL TIME: 10 MINS

These can be made ahead and kept in the fridge for up to five days for easy grab and go goodness! Or whip up a big punch bowl's worth for an acai bar at your next brunch/baby shower/ party. Just when you thought the superfood acai bowl could not get any better, this one has CHOCOLATE and MACA. If you're not on the maca bandwagon yet, you will be. Maca is an adaptogen that increases strength, energy, stamina aaaaaaand.... libido. Score!

GRANOLA: Combine all of the granola ingredients in a food processor, pulse to chop/ combine to a slightly chunky consistency. That's it - super easy.

ACAI MIX: Put all of the acai mix ingredients in a high-powered blender and blend smooth. Done.

MAKE THE ACAI BOWL: Add ½ cup of the granola mix in a bowl (the one you're serving it in), top with 1 cup of acai mix. Sprinkle more granola on top or add fresh fruit if you have any on hand. Get creative and make it uber #instaworthy with coconut flakes, goji berries, mango slices, fresh mint—the more colors of the rainbow the better.

Optional: drizzle with chocolate sauce

ADAPTOGEN:

noun: adaptogen; plural noun: adaptogens

a natural substance considered to help the body adapt to stress and to exert a normalizing effect upon bodily processes

THEY DON'T TASTE HEALTHY MUFFINS

½ cup cassava flour

¼ cup psyllium powder

¼ cup sacha inchi powder

2 teaspoons baking soda

½ teaspoon sea salt

4 tablespoons plant butter or
coconut oil

2 teaspoons cinnamon

2 (v)eggs (*see recipe on pg.
23*)

3 tablespoons vanilla

½ cup granulated sweetener
(*I like monk fruit*)

½ cup plant-based mayo
(*seriously!*)

4 ounces apple sauce

SERVES: 12
PREP TIME: 10 MINS | BAKE TIME: 30 MINS | TOTAL TIME: 40 MINS

Cardiologist approved, these delightful muffins are fluffy, flavorful and everything a muffin should be. And did I mention they're loaded with protein and fiber, and have zero gluten and sugar? Don't let the mayo freak you out. It makes these muffins soooo buttery. Trust me.

Preheat oven to 350 degrees.

Mix dry ingredients together in a large bowl.

In a separate bowl, whisk together all wet ingredients.

Add wet ingredients to dry and whisk until smooth.

Pour batter into lined and/or greased muffin tins and bake for 25-30 minutes, or until a toothpick comes out clean.

Remove from oven and let cool on wire rack before serving.

FLAVOR VARIATION ADD-INS:

BLUEBERRY: drop frozen or freeze-dried berries into each muffin tin before putting into oven.

LEMON POPPYSEED: add 1-2 tablespoons poppy seeds, 1 teaspoon lemon zest, and sub vanilla for 2:1 ratio lemon juice to vanilla.

CHOCOLATE: add in ½ cup cacao powder or ground cacao nibs.

CHOCOLATE CHIP: add in ½ cup of your fave chocolate chips.

PUMPKIN SPICE: replace apple sauce with pumpkin puree, add 1 tablespoon pumpkin pie spice.

CINNAMON SWIRL COFFEE CAKE

COFFEE CAKE

1 ½ cups almond flour

1 cup cassava flour

1 teaspoon ground cinnamon

1 teaspoon ground cardamom

½ teaspoon baking soda

¼ teaspoon sea salt

¼ teaspoon lemon zest

4 veggs (*see pg, 23.*)

¼ cup coconut oil (*melted to liquid - run jar under hot water*)

½ cup honey (*liquid*)

1 teaspoon vanilla extract

1 Granny Smith Apple, cored and chopped

1 Honey Crisp Apple, cored and chopped

SPICED SWIRL

1 ½ teaspoons cinnamon

1 ½ teaspoons cardamom

2 tablespoons honey (*liquid*)

½ tablespoon coconut oil (*melted*)

GLAZE

2 tablespoons coconut oil (*melted*)

2 tablespoons honey

2 tablespoons coconut cream (*buy the cream or chill full fat coconut milk and scoop the fat off the top*)

Pinch of cinnamon

SERVES: 12 *BUT I KNOW PEOPLE WHO HAVE EATEN HALF OF IT IN ONE SITTING.*
PREP TIME: 15 MINS | BAKE TIME: 35 MINS | SET TIME: 15 MINS | TOTAL TIME: 1 HR 5 MINS

*Plump and moist with a touch of sugar and spice, this cake melts in your mouth and hits all the right spots. I first made this cake around the holidays in 2008. I was pregnant with my oldest, newly diagnosed as being celiac and in need of some holiday flavor. It's so easy to make, and hard to f*ck up, you'll wonder how you lived this long without it.*

Preheat the oven to 350°F.

Mix all the dry cake ingredients together in a large bowl.

Add in the wet ingredients and mix well until a sticky dough forms.

Fold in the chopped apples.

Use coconut oil (or the spray kind) to lightly oil a Bundt cake pan. Pour the cake mix into the cake pan.

In a small bowl, stir together the spiced swirl ingredients.

Drizzle the swirl mix over the top of the cake. Next, drag a chopstick or knife (or even a kebab skewer - whatever you have) through the cake batter in swirly motions, letting the drizzle drip down into the cracks. I've even let my kids do this, it adds some swirly fun, but mostly delicious flavor strips.

Pop that baby into the oven (middle rack), and bake for 30 minutes.

After 30 minutes, turn off the oven and leave cake in the oven for 5 more minutes.

Remove and let cool for 15-20 minutes before removing from pan. The easiest way to do this is to get a plate that is just larger than your pan, and place it upside down over the pan. Holding the plate secure against the pan, flip it over, and you should feel the cake slip/plop onto the plate. Lift the pan off, and voilà!

Mix together the glaze ingredients and let sit on the counter at room temperature until ready to serve.

Drizzle glaze over the cake and serve.

CULT WORTHY YOGURT & PARFAIT

YOGURT

6 Young Thai Coconuts

2 teaspoons probiotic powder

¼ cup coconut oil, melted

MAKE IT A PARFAIT

1 cup berries

1 cup yogurt

2 tablespoon hemp seeds

2 tablespoon slivered almonds

TIP

HOW TO OPEN A COCONUT: There are a ton of YouTube tutorials on this if you've never done it before, and even specialty tools to jack open coconuts. I use a strong sharp paring knife and scrape the top part of the husk off (the point). This will reveal the circle in the brown shell of the coconut. Take that same knife, and stab three points in the circle like a triangle. You'll then be able to pry the top off. It may take some time at first, but once you get the hang of it, it's pretty easy and quick.

MAKES: 16 OZ
PREP TIME: 15 MINS | FERMENT TIME: 2 DAYS | TOTAL TIME: 2 DAYS 15 MINS

The combination of superior probiotics and this simple yogurt is guaranteed to fix your sh*t. Literally. This also makes an awesome dessert. Need an awesome probiotic powder? Two of my faves are Elemental Wizdom and Progurt.

Open the coconuts and reserve the water.

Use a slim spatula or spoon to scrape the coconut meat out.

Puree the coconut meat in a high powered blender or food processor, slowly add in the coconut water 1 tablespoon at a time until you reach the desired consistency. You'll have plenty of water left over to drink unless you prefer very runny yogurt.

While the blender or food processor is still running, slowly add in the coconut oil.

Pour the mixture into a 16 ounce mason jar. Stir in the probiotic powder and seal tight.

Allow the yogurt to ferment on your kitchen counter (ideal room temp around 74-78 F) for up to 48 hours.

<u>NOTE:</u> Make sure the jar is sealed very tight or it will explode all over your kitchen. No bueno. You've been warned.

Check after 12 hours, it should have a little bit of tartness/sourness to the taste. If you like your yogurt sweeter, you can stir in your sweetener of choice to taste now. Keep it in the fridge from now on, always being sure to re-seal it tightly. These are some kickass, highly active probiotics.

PARFAIT FOR 2: Layer ¼ cup of berries in the bottom of serving bowl and top with ¼ cup of the yogurt. Repeat with another ¼ cup of berries topped with another ¼ cup of yogurt. Finish with a sprinkling of hemp seeds and slivered almonds.

VEGGS PATTIES

1 cup chickpea flour

1 ½ cups water

1 pinch sea salt

1 tablespoon fresh chives, minced

1 teaspoon garlic powder/ granules

1 teaspoon onion powder/ granules

½ teaspoon kala namak salt (*find online or for cheap at your local asian grocer*)

¼ teaspoon turmeric (*mostly for color, but it does add some flavor*)

¼ teaspoon smoked paprika (*you can use reg, but I believe smoke is an underrated flavor*)

¼ teaspoon black pepper (*or mix it up with white!*)

Olive oil spray

MAKES: 6
PREP TIME: 5 MINS | COOK TIME: 5-10 MINS | SET TIME: 8 HRS | BAKE TIME: 10-12 MINS
TOTAL TIME: 8 HRS 20-32 MINS

These vegan egg substitutes—aka veggs— are so legit it pops up in several places in the book. Here you'll find how to make scrambled and pattie versions. If your heart is set on the quiche, you'll want to make the scramble version and basically smash it into the crust.

Preheat the oven to 425 degrees.

Bring 1 cup of water to a boil in a sauce pan, with a pinch of sea salt.

In a separate bowl, mix together ½ cup water with the chickpea flour, turmeric and paprika. It'll turn into a gunky paste.

Stir the gunky paste into the boiling water. Keep stirring. Seriously, don't stop, and pay attention so it doesn't sink and stick to the bottom of the pan. It's a minor pain in the arse, but so worth it.

Once thick and gloopy instead of gunky, remove from the heat and pour into a parchment lined and olive oil sprayed Pyrex.

Stir in all the remaining ingredients, mix well to combine, and refrigerate overnight (at least 8 hours).

Once set, use the parchment paper to lift the veggs out of the Pyrex. Use a cookie or biscuit cutter to cut out 6 round shapes. You can also do squares and use a pizza cutter or big knife to cut into 6 squares. If you're making a bunch of these in advance, you can freeze them in an airtight container and keep for up to two weeks in the freezer.

Place the shapes on a fresh parchment lined baking sheet, and bake for 10 minutes at 425 degrees to heat through. If you froze them, you can thaw in fridge or place directly on the parchment lined sheet and bake 10-12 minutes until hot.

VEGG SCRAMBLE

1 cup chickpea flour

1 ½ cups water

1 pinch sea salt

1 tablespoon fresh chives, minced

1 teaspoon garlic powder/ granules

1 teaspoon onion powder/ granules

½ teaspoon kala namak salt (*find online or for cheap at your local asian grocer*)

¼ teaspoon turmeric (*mostly for color, but it does add some flavor*)

¼ teaspoon smoked paprika (*you can use reg, but I believe smoke is an underrated flavor*)

¼ teaspoon black pepper (*or mix it up with white!*)

Olive oil spray

MAKES: 6
PREP TIME: 5 MINS | COOK TIME: 5-10 MINS | TOTAL TIME: 10-15 MINS

Bring 1 cup of water to a boil in a sauce pan with a pinch of sea salt.

In a separate bowl, mix together ½ cup water with the chickpea flour, turmeric and paprika. It'll turn into a gunky paste.

Stir the gunky paste into the boiling water. Keep stirring. Seriously, don't stop, and pay attention so it doesn't sink and stick to the bottom of the pan. It's a minor pain in the arse, but so worth it.

Once thick and gloopy instead of gunky, add in whatever things the recipe needs (like sausage/vacon, cheese and salsa in the breakfast tacos), and stir to form a scramble.

If you're not adding anything, just scramble it around with a spatula, or utensil of choice. Here's where you can also add buttah, salt and pepper, or your own creative twist.

TIP:

The black salt, Kala Namak, has a high sulfur taste to it, so a little goes a long, long, long way. So don't add extra hoping for an extra egg flavor. Most ingredients in my recipes can be estimated, leaving room for, let's say creativity instead of error. But, the margin for error with the kala namak is small. It's potent AF. It's the key to the egg flavor, so if you opt for plant eggs because you don't like egg flavor, skip the kala namak salt.

VACON

2 zucchinis, thinly sliced into strips (*OR 1 eggplant, sliced in half, then cut into ¼ inch strips and chopped to bits for bacon bits. They shrink when cooking so don't chop too small*)

8 tablespoons EVOO (*extra virgin olive oil*)

4 tablespoons maple syrup

4 tablespoons apple cider vinegar

2 tablespoons liquid smoke (*yup, bacon is smoky*)

1 teaspoon sea salt (*yes, that much, bacon is salty*)

Black pepper to taste

1 teaspoon oil for cooking

SERVES: 4
PREP TIME: 5-10 MINS | MARINADE TIME: 10-15 MINS | COOK TIME: 5 MINS | TOTAL TIME: 20-30 MINS

Why do we bake cookies, and cook bacon? That's not a joke. Sorry for vacon your heart, I couldn't come up with any plant bacon puns for this, no matter how hard I fried.

———————

Pat the zucchini/eggplant strips or bits dry with a clean paper/dish towel. Don't skip this step, you want these little guys thirsty, so they soak up all the marinade.

Place all ingredients except the cooking oil in a container, stir to mix, and let sit for 10-15 minutes. That's the ideal range. Less time doesn't allow the strips to soak enough goodness, and too much time makes them mushy and impossible to work with.

Heat the cooking oil in a skillet over medium-high heat, and then fry the vacon strips or bits for about 2 minutes.

Flip the strips or shake up the bits and continue frying another couple of minutes until they begin to crisp/firm.

Transfer to a towel lined plate (paper or cloth, your choice, make sure it's clean), and let the excess oil drain while it cools.

BREAKFAST SAUSAGE

2 cups walnuts

2 cups sunflower seeds

1 cup portobello mushrooms, chopped/minced

½ cup flaxseed

¼ cup onion, minced (*yellow or red, mix it up!*)

2 cloves garlic

3 tablespoons sage (*2 TB if using dried, 1 TB if powdered*)

1 tablespoon Italian seasoning

1 tablespoon red chili flakes

1 teaspoon cumin powder

2 tablespoons maple syrup

Black pepper to taste

Sea salt to taste

SERVES: 4
PREP TIME: 2 MINS | COOK TIME: 0-5 MINS | TOTAL TIME: 2-7 MINS

Throw all ingredients in a food processor and process until it has a ground sausage consistency.

For patties, ball up and flatten into hockey puck disks to fry.

For ground, heat in a skillet.

For recipes in this book, follow recipe (like toss in with your eggs to heat).

CASSAVA TORTILLAS

1 ½ cups cassava flour

½ teaspoon sea salt

4 tablespoons oil (*olive/ avocado/savory*)

⅔ cup lukewarm water (*not hot, not cold*)

SERVES: 4
PREP TIME: 5 MINS | COOK TIME: 16 MINS | TOTAL TIME: 21 MINS

Ever curl up in bed with a fresh cup of hot tea or coffee while rain falls outside the windows because you have nowhere to go and nothing to do? Yeah me neither... BUT, these tortillas remind of that common parent fantasy. They're like a cozy blanket for your insides, but one you can stuff and spread with food and not have to do laundry ASAP!

Combine flour and salt in a bowl.

Add in lukewarm water and oil, kneading into a big dough ball.

Divide into two equal balls. Repeat dividing until you have a total of eight equal sized dough balls.

Place one ball on a sheet of parchment paper, top with another sheet of parchment, and roll out the ball into a pretty, wide, round and thin tortilla.

Heat a non stick skillet over medium-high heat. Do NOT add any liquid/steam/oil/moisture/etc. You will need a dry skillet.

Once nice and hot, place a tortilla on the skillet and wait for bubbles to form, about 1 minute. Flip and cook the other side for 1 minute.

If you don't have a tortilla warmer, place the tortillas on a plate and cover with another plate, or a clean and dry dish towel, stacking the tortillas under it to keep each other warm and cozy.

JESSICA'S FAMOUS FLUFFY PANCAKES

1½ cups gluten-free flour
(*make your own with 1 cup
cassava flour and ½ cup
almond flour*)

3 tablespoons sweetener (*I
like monk fruit*)

2 teaspoons baking powder

1 ½ teaspoons sea salt

½ cup cream cheese

¾ cup plant milk

2 (v)eggs (see pg. 23)

2 teaspoons vanilla extract

1 teaspoon lemon zest

1 pinch ground cardamom

FOR COOKING

Vegan butter (*Miyokos
Kitchen has an amazing
European Style one -100%
plant based*)

FOR GARNISH

Vegan butter

Maple Syrup (*splurge on the
100% pure!*)

Lemon zest

SERVES: 4
PREP TIME: 5 MINS | COOK TIME: 10 MINS | TOTAL TIME: 15 MINS

These are the absolute best pancakes I've ever made in my life, and likely the only ones I'll ever make until the day I die. If you don't have cardamom on hand, you can omit it, or even swap out the lemon zest for chocolate chips if that's your thing. But, try it straight up first. If you could eat happiness, that's what these taste like.

Combine all dry ingredients together in a bowl and whisk to incorporate.

In a separate bowl, whisk together all wet ingredients.

Add wet ingredients to dry and whisk smooth. You can use a mixer too. The batter is a little too thick for a blender though, and you don't want to waste any by getting it stuck in the blades.

Heat a large skillet to medium-low and add a bit of butter. After the butter melts and begins to bubble, it's time to spoon/pour the batter in. My skillet is large enough to make four 4-5" pancakes at a time. Do what works in your pan.

When pancakes begin to bubble, about 2-3 minutes, flip them and cook the other side. After another 2-3 minutes, remove from pan and serve.

If you're like me, and want to serve everyone at once, stack the pancakes on top of each other with a clean dish towel to keep warm, OR preheat the oven to the lowest setting, turn it off, and then hold them in the oven until all are cooked.

Place pancakes on each plate, top with a beautiful blob of butter, a generous drizzle of maple syrup and a sprinkling of lemon zest.

PUFF PASTRY CRUST

2 cups cassava flour (*or sub any gluten free flour blend*)

1 teaspoon starch (*I like arrowroot starch*)

¾ teaspoon sea salt

4 tablespoons cold buttah or coconut oil (*solid, very cold*), cut in chunks

½ cup water

½ cup ice cubes

¼ cup ice cold water

FOR BUTTAH PACK

8 ounces semi soft butter or coconut oil

½ cup cassava flour (*or same gluten free blend as above*) for dusting

MAKES: 2 PASTRY CRUSTS
TOTAL TIME: 45-60 MINS, BUT WORTH EVERY SECOND

This is a great and easy recipe to get kids into the kitchen. There are no knives or heat, and they can squish and roll and "paint" the dough! Plus, they learn fractions when folding in thirds, and patience when waiting the 8-10 minutes. Everybody wins.

Preheat oven to 325 degrees.

In a food processor, pulse together the flour, starch and sea salt.

While still pulsing, add the chunks of butter or coconut oil, pulsing until crumbly texture. Be careful not to pulse too long. We don't want the butter or coconut oil to melt.

Dump the mixture into a large bowl and use your hand to create a well in the middle.

Add the ice cubes to the ½ cup of water to make it ice cold.

Pour the ½ cup of ice cold water (not the ice cubes) into the flour mix well. Stir the mixture to combine.

Slowly add the ¼ cup of ice water 1 tablespoon at a time until the dough stays together when pressed. It will have a nice Play-Doh like consistency, but it'll likely smell better, because . . . butter.

Form the dough into a ball, wrap it up air tight in plastic wrap (eek, I know... not sustainable but works the best) and place in the fridge to chill while prepping the next steps.

Place parchment paper down on a half sheet pan (13" x 18" - probably what you have in your home already), and lightly dust the pan with flour.

Remove the dough ball from the fridge, unwrap it, and press it into a round disc on the prepared sheet pan surface. Sprinkle the top of the dough disc with a light dusting of flour.

Roll the dough out into a large rectangle about the size of the sheet pan, and ¼" thick.

Smear an even layer of the slightly softened buttah or coconut oil across the top of the dough. You should be using ¼ cup (2 ounces) of the butter/coconut oil.

Carefully fold the dough in thirds, raising the short ends over the center on itself like a letter. Think trifold snail mail.

Smear with 2 more tablespoons of butter or coconut oil.

Fold the rectangle in thirds again, short side over center and other short side over the folded short side over the center. Again, like a snail mail letter, except now the dough will look almost square.

You've just created a bunch of delicious buttah-ry flaky pastry layers! Good job! BUT, we need more to make it even better. More is definitely more here. Carefully wrap your beautiful puff to be in the plastic wrap and pop the dough back in the fridge to keep the butter (or coconut oil) from melting and combining with the dough. Let it chill until the butter/coconut oil is hard, about 8-10 minutes.

Remove the dough from the fridge and we will repeat the flaky making fun. Re-dust the baking sheet with flour, place the dough on top, dust with a little more flour, and roll it back out into a big rectangle again.

Smear with another even layer of about ¼ cup (2 ounces) of the melty butter/semi-solid coconut oil.

Carefully fold the dough on itself in thirds (trifold like a letter).

Slather another 2 tablespoons of butter/coconut oil on top.

Fold the long skinny rectangle in thirds again so it's more of a small square shape again. It's TWICE as flaky now! Woohoo! However, this is about as flaky as a store bought gluten free croissant. No bueno. We can, and will, do much better so let's continue.

Carefully wrap that dough back up in the plastic wrap (keep using the same sheet), and place it back in the fridge to keep those buttah-ry doughy layers separate. Let it chill for another 8-10 minutes.

Dust the sheet pan again and remove the dough from the fridge, unwrap it and place it back on the sheet pan. Redust the top and roll it back out to the size of the pan, slathering in butter/coconut oil again, folding in thirds again, slathering in buttah/coconut oil again, and folding in thirds again so it's back to that square-ish shape.

Repeat steps 22 & 23 - TWO MORE TIMES. I promise it is worth it. Don't skip the fridge time. Don't skip the extra butter/coconut oil layers. Wrap it back up in the plastic wrap and place it back in the fridge to chill for 8-10 minutes when done.

Remove the dough from the fridge and divide it in two. If you're not using the dough now, you can store it in the fridge for a week in an airtight container. It'll keep in the freezer for up to 6 weeks! When you want to use it, defrost in the fridge overnight.

BUTTERMILK BISCUITS

1 cup cassava flour

1 cup almond flour

½ cup plant milk (*never soy, almond best*)

2 tablespoons same plant milk

3 tablespoons buttah or coconut oil, slightly melted, soft but not liquid best

2 tablespoons arrowroot starch

1 tablespoon lemon juice (*fresh is always best*)

1 ¼ teaspoons cream of tartar (*not a cream, a white powder in the baking section*)

1 ¼ teaspoons baking soda

½ teaspoon sea salt

FOR BISCUIT "EGG WASH"

2 tablespoons coconut oil or buttah (*also slightly mushy/ melty consistency*)

1 tablespoon plant milk (*not soy, flavor and texture no bueno*)

MAKES: 6 - 8 DEPENDING ON SIZE OF BISCUIT CUTTER OR GLASS RIM
PREP TIME: 10-15 MINS | COOK TIME: 17 MINS | TOTAL TIME: 27-32 MINS

My kids inspire me to create new recipes - that's the nice way of saying they demand & persuade me into making a specific food to try because they never had it due to someone's food allergy or intolerance. Like these biscuits.

One saturday morning the boys are watching classic cartoons,while I'm making breakfast. My then 5 year old comes running into the kitchen and tells me I "have to make buttermilk biscuits" for him right now, because he's never tried them before. He throws his arms around my legs and hugs me tight then proceeds to tell me that if I make them right now, then not only am I the most "beautifullest mommy ever" but also the nicest AND the sweetest AND the very best mommy ever.

That kid was born knowing how to win friends and influence people. Being a sucker for his puppy dog eyes, big smile, tight hugs and thickly layered flattery, I got to work on making his food fantasies a reality.

Preheat the oven to 425 degrees.

In a mixing bowl, combine all the wet ingredients except the buttah/coconut oil.

Place a mesh colander or sieve over a large mixing bowl, and dump all the dry ingredients in it, shaking through so the flour mix is nice and fluffy. Don't skip this, gluten free doesn't have gluten (duh) so it's easy to make it dense. The fluffier your flour mix, the better.

Add buttah/coconut oil to the dry ingredients and whisk/fork it to cut the flour into the mix.

Add the wet ingredient mix to the flour mix and whisk/fork until combined.

Dust a work surface with cassava flour, transfer the dough to the floured surface and press it out into 1 ½ to 2" thickness. No need to bother with a rolling pin, hands work perfectly for this. These are gluten free, so they're not going to rise a bunch. Take care not to flatten them out too much (another reason to skip the rolling pin).

Using a well floured biscuit cutter—or rim of a drinking glass, whatever you have—cut out 6 to 8 biscuits. If you can get more than that, you probably flattened your dough too much. It's okay, you can use them as halves instead of cutting them in half later.

Place each biscuit on a parchment lined baking sheet. Don't grease the sheet, the bottoms will burn. Whoops.

Mix the 2 tablespoons of buttah/coconut oil and 1 tablespoon of almond milk together then brush the top of each biscuit with the mix so they get those delicious golden tops. If you have a pastry brush, go for it. I have one, and still end up using my hands, a spoon, or even a clean dish cloth half the time.

Bake for 15 minutes until slightly risen.

Crank up the oven temperature to 475 degrees for 2 minutes to really develop those golden tops. Keep an eye on them, they're the avocado of carbs: not yet, not yet, perfection, ruined.

Enjoy on their own, bathed in buttah, or in one of the recipes in this book (like my breakfast sandwich on pg. 42).

BREAKFAST TACOS

Cassava tortillas (*pg. 28*)

Scrambled Veggs (*pg.23*)

Breakfast Sausage (*pg. 25*)

Vacon (*pg. 24*)

SALSA ROJA INGREDIENTS

3 medium tomatoes, de-stemmed

½ cup cilantro, packed (*that means stuff it all down into the measuring cup, more is always better when it comes to cilantro*)

2 cloves garlic

1 jalapeno pepper, de-stemmed (*def de-seed if you can't take the heat*)

1 serrano pepper, de-stemmed (*remove the seeds for no heat*)

1 lime, peeled

1 tablespoon nutritional flakes (*technically optional, but highly recommended*)

MIX-INS

Shredded pepper jack or cheddar flavored plant based cheese

GARNISH

Fresh chopped cilantro

Fresh squeeze of lime

Spicy sauce (*Tabasco, Chohula, or pick your poison*)

MAKES: 8
TOTAL TIME: 30 -60 MINS, DEPENDS ON IF YOU MAKE THE PARTS AT ONCE OR CONSECUTIVELY

In queso you were wondering, while you can't trust most tacos (they tend to spill the beans), you CAN trust this taco to be absolutely spec-taco-ler.

Make the vacon (pg. 24)

Make the sausage (pg. 25)

Make the veggs (pg. 23)

Make the tortillas (pg. 28)

Spice it up: throw all the salsa ingredients in a food processor (yes, really, the whole lime), and pulse to your desired consistency.

Put it all together: place a tortilla on a plate, place half a cup of the vegg mix on top, as much or as little salsa as you want, add any mix-ins and garnishes, roll up and enjoy. OR set up a taco bar. This lets people build their ideal taco, and lets you chill, it's a win-win.

Finally, let's taco 'bout how to eat a taco gracefully:

Step 1: Pick up taco with both hands

Step 2: Tilt your head, to either side, not front or back, at least 45 degrees, no more than 90, I find 55-60 degrees to be the sweet spot.

Step 3: Smile, you'll look less silly taking a massive bite. This step is easy, because tacos make everybody smile.

Step 4: Don't fret, you can rest assured you won't be eating a taco gracefully. Especially first thing in the morning. Tacos are not about grace, they're about flavor and fun!

QUICHE LORRAINE

1 Puff Pastry crust (*pg. 32*)

1 veggs scramble (*pg. 23*)

1 vacon (*optional - pg. 24, sundried tomatoes also make a nice salty substitute*)

A bit of cassava or gluten free flour blend for dusting work surface

1 cup spinach or leafy greens of choice, chopped (*you really want to use fresh here, you can use frozen in a pinch, but needs to be completely thawed, drained and pat as dry as possible*)

1 cup shredded provolone, gruyere or gouda flavored plant cheese

½ cup shallots, sliced

2 tablespoons savory oil (*olive, infused, avocado, etc, can even use buttah*)

SERVES: 6
PREP TIME: 30 MINS | COOK TIME: 20 MINS | CHILL TIME: 45 MINS | TOTAL TIME: 1 HR 35 MINS

This will undoubtedly be your favorite brunch dish. You might even want to make two! I've served this as well as a traditional ingredient quiche at many family holiday gatherings, and this gluten free, dairy free, egg free one is always gone first! It's one of the recipes, when telling people I was writing this book, that got a resounding "you have to put that quiche in it!" The puff pastry can be made up to 6 weeks in advance. We start cranking them out at our house on the weekends in the fall to have plenty stocked up for the holiday season.

———————————

Preheat the oven to 325 degrees

Remove your puff pastry dough from the fridge, place on a flour dusted work surface and quickly roll out the dough into the shape of your quiche pan, and slightly larger than the quiche pan so the crust can go up the edges. For most pans, you'll want to go about two fingers width wider than your pan. Try to move fast and not touch the dough too much with your hands so the buttah/coconut oil doesn't melt into the dough layers.

Carefully lift the dough and place over your quiche pans, letting it sink down in to the bottom, while quickly using your finger tips to lay the dough around the walls of the pan.

Place the quiche crust and pan back in the fridge and chill until ready to fill.

For the filling, heat 2 tablespoons of oil in a large skillet over medium heat. Toss in the shallots and saute until they begin to caramelize, about 5 minutes.

In a medium bowl, mix together the vegg scramble, vacon (if using), caramelized shallots, greens and cheese flavored shreds, to combine.

Remove the quiche pans from the fridge, and scoop the filling into the pan, pressing it in so it's packed firmly.

Bake for 10 minutes until all the cheesy parts are melted and the crust starts to golden.

Remove from the oven and let cool for 3-5 minutes before serving.

SAUSAGE SCRAMBLE WITH BURST TOMATOES

1 sausage recipe (*pg. 25*)

1 veggs recipe (*pg. 23*)

3 cups grape or cherry tomatoes

3 tablespoons olive oil

Sea salt to taste

Fresh pepper to taste

1 tablespoon savory oil for cooking

FOR GARNISH

4 tablespoons chives, chopped (*speed it up, use scissors to cut into small bits*)

½ cup plant based cream cheese (*You can also simply add these to the skillet at the end. It won't be as pretty, but sometimes the slightly warmed cream cheese is especially nice.*)

SERVES: 4
PREP TIME: 15 MINS | COOK TIME: 16 MINS | TOTAL TIME: 21 MINS

In a large skillet, heat the 3 tablespoons of olive oil over medium-high heat.

Very carefully add in the tomatoes (watch out for oil splatters). Season with salt and pepper, stirring occasionally to coat all the tomatoes and encourage bursting. Cook for 3-5 minutes until the tomatoes begin to shrivel.

Add the sausage mix, stirring carefully to mix, but not smash the tomatoes. Cook for 1 minute.

Add in the veggs, stirring carefully to combine, still trying not to smash those tomatoes, which should be on the verge of bursting by now. Cook for 1-2 minutes.

Plate and garnish with chopped chives and a dollop of cream cheese.

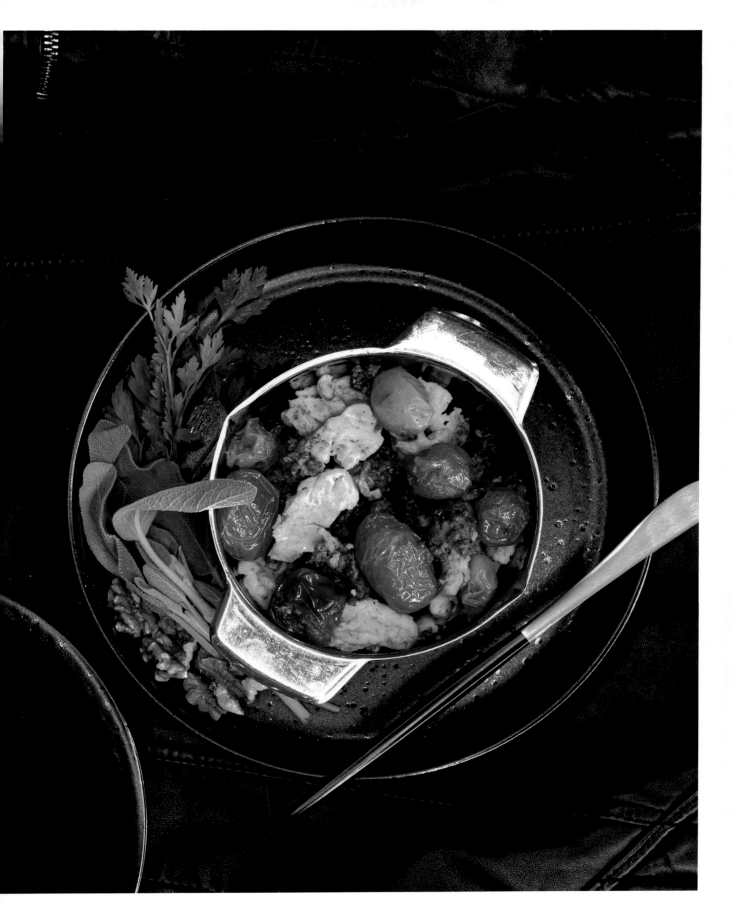

YUMMY BREAKFAST SANDWICH

Sausage (*pg. 25*)

Veggs as patties (*pg. 22*)

Buttermilk biscuits (*pg. 34*)

TRIMMINGS

1 slice American flavor
cheese (*trust me on this*)

1 drizzle of honey

Minced chives

Drizzle of spicy sauce
(*Chohula, Tabasco, Sriracha,
Louisiana style, etc.*)

SERVES: 4
PREP TIME: 10 MINS | CHILL TIME: 10 MINS | TOTAL TIME: 20 MINS

I'm not yolking when I say no eggsistential crisis here. Real talk, this sammy is eggcellent. I crack myself up... That's all yolks, thanks a brunch!

Preheat oven to 350 degrees.

Slice biscuit in half, spread coconut oil or vegan butter on ONE half of bread.

Place both halves cut side up on a wire rack on a baking sheet.

On the non-slathered half, place one slice of American flavor vegan cheese. Top with one vegan sausage patty

On the slathered bread, fold over the thin chickpea scramble.

Bake for 8-10 minutes until cheese melts, and all has warmed.

Remove from oven, and drizzle egg side with a bit of honey and spicy sauce, close sandwich halves together. Serve and/or scarf down.

SOUPS

MAGIC DETOX "POOP" SOUP

2 cups carrot coins - or chopped carrots

2 cups celery, sliced or chopped

1 bunch radishes, sliced

2 zucchinis, sliced and cut in quarters

2 parsnips, sliced and cut in half circles

2 beets (any color), sliced and cut in quarters

1/4 cup chopped cilantro

1/4 cup chopped parsley

2 tablespoons oil (olive, avocado, MCT, your choice)

2 tablespoons lime juice

1 teaspoon black pepper

1/4 teaspoon sea salt

2 bags dandelion tea

GARNISH

sliced avocado

fresh cilantro, chopped

fresh parsley, chopped

fresh lime juice (to squeeze on top)

SERVES: 2
PREP TIME: 10 MINS | COOK TIME: 20-30 MINS | TOTAL TIME: 30-40 MINS

Don't let the name discourage you. This soup is a winner. I make this in big batches and keep in the fridge all winter long. It started off as just an awesome detox soup, to reset the palette and load the body with the nutrients it needs to run better, particularly after too many holiday parties, or overdoing it at Thanksgiving. Friends come over anytime I make this and request bowls to take home with them too! I always just assumed they REALLY liked the taste, or maybe the free hot meal. One day, a friend was over and I began cutting and prepping veggies for the soup, he says, "Oh hey! Are you making the poop soup? If I go buy more of this stuff can you make some for me, too?" It turns out, in addition to being delicious, it uhm… helps get the plumbing back on track.

Put all ingredients in a stock pot/crock pot/large saucepan and cover with water plus 2".

Bring to a boil and simmer, at least 20 minutes or up to an hour depending how soft you like your veggies.

Garnish with avocado slices, chopped herbs and a squeeze of lime juice. This will keep in the fridge for 3-5 days. Simply pour it into a pot on the stove over medium heat to reheat.

HEARTY + HEALTHY LENTIL SOUP

2 ½ cups celery, cut in chunks

2 ½ cups carrots, cut in chunks

1 medium yellow onion, quartered

3 tablespoon oil (*I like avocado oil for this*)

3 cloves garlic, minced

1 medium shallot, sliced

1/4 teaspoon sea salt

1/4 teaspoon black pepper

2 cups diced tomato (*fresh or canned, no sodium*)

1 tablespoon tarragon

1 tablespoon oregano

1 tablespoon thyme

6 quarts water (*or broth if you have, but not needed*)

4 cups lentils (*I like sprouted french green, any but red/yellow works - those get mushy*)

3 bay leaves

1 ½ cups wine (*OPTIONAL: I almost always opt for a dry white wine to cook*)

GARNISH

balsamic vinegar

olive oil

black pepper

fresh herbs

SERVES: 4-6
PREP TIME: 10 MINS | COOK TIME: 34 MINS | TOTAL TIME: 45 MINS

This is the only lentil recipe you'll ever need. I like it best with a dry white wine, but it's just as good with red wine, a wine vinegar or naked (the soup, that is). Use whatever you have on hand!

To prep the veggies, pulse celery, carrots and onion in your food processor until finely chopped and well combined (or buy them pre chopped at the grocery store's prepped food section and measure out 2 cups celery, 2 cups carrot and a 1/2 cup onion).

Heat the oil in a large (8 or more quart) soup pot on med-high heat, add garlic, shallot, sea salt and pepper.

Add in diced tomatoes, tarragon, oregano and thyme, and then stir.

Add in prepped veggies, 6 quarts of water, 4 cups lentils, and 3 bay leaves. Stir and bring to a boil.

Reduce heat to simmer. If using wine, add it in now, and cook covered for 30 min, stirring occasionally.

The liquid will reduce greatly. When done stir and serve, drizzle with balsamic vinegar and olive oil, and sprinkle with black pepper. Crusty bread optional, but highly recommended.

EASY CREAMY TOMATO BASIL SOUP

1 - 32 ounce jar of your favorite marinara (*I love spicy, basil and garlic flavors*)

1 - 8 ounce container soft plant-based cheese (*french style or cream best, flavored or not*)

½ cup roasted garlic cloves

½ cup olive oil

¼ cup chopped fresh basil

VEG PARMESAN

1 cup raw nuts (*brazil, walnuts, or macadamia*)

1/4 cup nutritional flakes

1 tablespoon garlic powder

1 teaspoon sea salt

GARNISH

fresh basil

veg parmesan

SERVES: 2
PREP TIME: 10 MINS | COOK TIME: 20-30 MINS | TOTAL TIME: 30-40 MINS

I love a good creamy tomato basil soup, especially when scooping it up with grilled cheese. My grandma (she was actually my great grandmother) used to make tomato soup and grilled cheese for us when we'd visit as kids. This one is a lot fancier, and has a richer taste than the Campbell's soup she made. But, it is just as easy to make. Score!

Process all the parmesan ingredients together in a food processor until crumbly and fluffy like parmesan. Keeps in fridge for 6 weeks.

In a medium saucepan over medium heat, heat all ingredients together, stirring to incorporate the creamy cheese. If you're in a hurry, pulse the soup in the blender to combine "cheese" quicker.

Cook 20-30 minutes to let all the flavors meld together. You can technically just blend this in the blender on high for 5 minutes, to warm it up, and eat it that way. The flavors will still be there, but not quite as much depth as cooking it slowly. The kids can't tell a difference either way, and love making it in the blender.

Garnish with chopped basil and veg parmesan.

NOTE:

Not necessary at all, but if you feel like mixing it up, a ¼ cup of a nice heavier red, like Shiraz or Chianti can be quite nice. But, you will really need to cook it for the full 30 minutes if going that route.

GREAT GREEN GAZPACHO

13 cups cucumber puree/pulp
(*leftover from juicing or run
through the food processor*)

3 cups tomatillo, pureed

½ cup avocado, mashed

¼ cup olive oil

2 tablespoons chopped fresh
cilantro

1 tablespoon lime juice

1 tablespoon garlic powder
(*or 2 cloves*)

1 teaspoon diced jalapeño
or Serrano (*remove seeds if
you're not a spicy fan, double
if you like more*)

½ tsp sea salt

GARNISH

Avocado slices

Fresh herbs (*cilantro, parsley
or mint*)

Chopped onions (*red look
prettiest*)

Lime squeeze

SERVES: 6-8
PREP TIME: 5 MINS | COOK TIME: 15 MINS | TOTAL TIME: 20 MINS

I loved soup as a kid, I wish I'd known about gazpacho! Although, I would pour salsa into a bowl and eat it like soup, so maybe I did. I simply didn't have the proper name for it.

———————

Mix all ingredients together in a big bowl and stir to combine. Garnish as you like. My usual garnishes are listed on this page. It's just as delicious without.

The garnish is more for #foodgoals if you photograph before you eat.

If you can refrain from devouring it all, it keeps in the fridge (in an airtight container) for 3-5 days before fermentation starts. After fermentation, consume at your own risk!

BLENDER BUTTERNUT SQUASH SOUP

1 pound butternut squash, cubed (*you can sub fresh for frozen and thawed, or even grab a BPA free can of puree*)

2 inch chunk of turmeric (*or 1 heaping teaspoon of powder*)

1 ½ cups water

1 bell pepper (*red*)

2 dates, pitted

1 teaspoon cumin

1 tablespoon olive oil

1 tablespoon lemon juice

Optional herbs: parsley, sage, rosemary and thyme (*use all three if you sing the song!*), or tarragon.

GARNISH

Avocado slices

Sweet Bell Peppers

Sesame Seeds

SERVES: 4-6
PREP TIME: 5 MINS | COOK TIME: 15 MINS | TOTAL TIME: 20 MINS

Sometimes I like cooking soup all day. The aromas waft through the house, gradually developing, building and deepening over hours. A sort of scentual foreplay for the moment when you sit down to dine, pick up the spoon in anticipation of the creamy flavor explosions in your mouth that warm you from the inside out until you're deeply satisfied. Other times I want it five minutes ago with minimal effort, but still tasting amazing, obviously. This does that. Well, not the time travel bit of it arriving 5 minutes ago, but you can definitely have it five minutes from when you start the blender!

This is where this recipe gets tricky. Just kidding. It's super easy. My 4 year old can make it on his own, as long as he remembers to put the lid on the blender. Ceiling soup is no bueno.

Place all ingredients in a high powered blender and puree smooth. Blend another 5 minutes until warm. That's it!

For #instaworthy level soup, add a bit of the fresh herbs for garnish and maybe sprinkle some seeds. Just be sure to tag me when you post.

If your blender isn't going to survive blending for five minutes, pour it in a pot on the stove and heat it over medium heat for about five minutes, until warm.

COCONUT CURRY IN A HURRY

1 - 16 ounce can coconut milk (*BPA free*)

1 - 4 ounce package frozen coconut meat (or ½ cup shredded, unsweetened)

1 tablespoon curry spice

1 tablespoon coconut oil

2 scoops protein powder (*optional*)

GARNISH

Diced red bell pepper

Avocado slices

Julienned carrots

Pumpkin seeds

SERVES: 2
PREP TIME: 5 MINS | COOK TIME: 5 MINS | TOTAL TIME: 10 MINS

Similar to what we make at my restaurant, this version is much easier, but still uber yummy. You can always make your own coconut milk by cracking open coconuts and blending it with some of the coconut water to desired thickness. I've found that the right balance is 1 cup coconut meat plus a blender's worth of coconut water. Blend the coconut meat with only a cup of the coconut water to get it super smooth and creamy, and then add the rest of the coconut water to fill the blender.

Place all ingredients in a high powered blender and puree smooth. We serve our version cold at the restaurant, I like this version both cold and hot.

To heat it, keep blending for about 5 minutes, or heat stovetop over medium heat until warm.

CHEAT:

Make it EVEN FASTER. If you have an instant hot water heater, use that water when blending it and you'll cut your cook time in half!

SLAM: SOUP (OF) LEEKS, ARTICHOKES + MUSHROOMS

2 leeks, sliced lengthwise and chopped into coins

2 big bay leaves (or 3-4 smaller, just remember how many because you can't eat them)

1 full sprig of thyme

¼ cup butter

1 pint crimini mushrooms, sliced (can sub baby bello, but crimini are my go to for this)

1 shallot, sliced

8 ounces of frozen artichoke heart quarters

12 ounces dry white wine (can use water or veg broth)

¼ teaspoon dried garlic granules (can use powder in a pinch)

¼ teaspoon dried onion granules (can sub powder if no granules)

¼ teaspoon dried parsley flakes

¼ teaspoon sea salt

SERVES: 4
PREP TIME: 5 MINS | COOK TIME: 1 HR TO 1 HR 30 MINS | TOTAL TIME: 1HR 5 MINS TO 1 HR 35 MINS

The French have a saying "faire le poireu." Literally translated, it means "to make the leek". What the expression really means is "to wait forever". Done properly, leeks take a while. Not "forever" but quite some time. Take my word for it, the time needed is totally worth it. Not only will you end up with Heaven in a bowl, but your home will smell divine while this soup is cooking.

In a medium pot - the one you'll be making the soup in - heat the butter over medium heat. Add the leeks and shallots and cook for 5 minutes.

Add the garlic, onion, parsley, sea salt, bay leaves and thyme. Cook for 15 more minutes.

Add the mushrooms and saute for 6 minutes, stirring to mix the mushrooms into the butter and spice goodness.

Add the artichoke hearts, continue to cook and stir occasionally for 6 more minutes.

Add the wine (or water or broth), cover and reduce heat to a simmer. Cook for at least 20 minutes, but no more than an hour. If serving to kids, add 12 ounces of water or broth and cook for an additional 30 minutes to burn off the alcohol in the wine.

Remove the thyme and bay leaves. Serve with crusty baguette slices.

Optional: This soup doubles as an absolutely delicious tapenade. To make, simply cook out or drain the excess liquid, and pulse the soup veggies in a food processor a few rounds until chunky. Serve warm alongside a soft plant based cheese, crusty bread, fresh or dried figs, raspberries and even honeycomb for a simple yet divine hors d'oeuvres spread.

NOTE:

I highly recommend a Sancerre or Chablis. They're dry and add some citrus notes while enhancing the earthiness of the soup and balancing the butter's richness. You can use a Sauvignon Blanc, too, if it's easier to find.

SALADS

ANYTHING BUT BASIC DINNER SALAD

1 pound mixed greens

1 tablespoon lemon juice

2 tablespoons olive oil

1 tablespoon hemp seeds

1 tablespoon nutritional flakes (*optional, but highly recommended*)

1 pinch sea salt, to taste

ADD-INS

Fresh ground black pepper

Toasted almonds

Pumpkin seeds

SERVES: 4-6
PREP TIME: 5 MINS | TOTAL TIME: 5 MINS

The only side salad you will ever need. It seriously goes with everything. Also, it's great after a meal to cleanse the palate before dessert or a cheese and fruit platter.

———————————

Toss all of the ingredients together in a large bowl until the greens are well coated.

Add in any optional add ins: fresh ground black pepper, toasted almonds or sprouted pumpkin seeds

WATERMELON SALAD

4 cups watermelon, cubed

2 large avocados, diced

1 pint cherry tomatoes, halved

½ cup fresh basil leaves, loosely packed

¼ cup fresh mint leaves, loosely packed

DRESSING

½ cup fresh squeezed orange juice

¼ cup fresh squeezed lemon juice

1 teaspoon shallot, minced

pinch sea salt

fresh ground pepper

SERVES: 2-4
PREP TIME: 5 MINS | TOTAL TIME: 5 MINS

So fresh, so good, so easy. This salad is both filling and hydrating on a hot summer's day, or any-time you can get watermelon! The first time I made it was for a last minute 4th of July potluck. I simply threw together things from the fridge and it was a huge hit!

_____

Mix all of the dressing ingredients together. If the shallot weirds you out, whiz the ingredients smooth in the blender, but don't leave it out.

Toss the dressing and salad ingredients together in a bowl and serve.

CARBS

ULTIMATE BAKED MAC-N-CHEESE

2 ½ cups butternut squash

½ cup milk of choice (I like almond)

½ cup nutritional yeast

¼ cup parmesan cheese

2 tablespoons oil (avocado, olive, or coconut)

2 cloves garlic, minced (about 1 tablespoon)

1 ½ tablespoons fresh sage, chopped (or 1 teaspoon dried)

1 ½ tablespoons fresh thyme, de-stemmed (or 1 teaspoon dried)

Sea salt to taste

Black pepper to taste

Red pepper to taste (Optional)

½ teaspoon truffle, oil, or avocado oil (Optional)

1 box pasta (I go gluten-free and love chickpea based pasta)

OPTIONAL

½ cup shredded cheddar flavor cheese (still delicious without)

½ cup shredded gouda flavor cheese (or double down on cheddar)

½ cup cream cheese (makes the absolute creamiest mac-n-cheese)

SERVES: 4-6
PREP TIME: 10 MINS | COOK TIME: 5-10 MINS | TOTAL TIME: 15-20 MINS

I went to a Montessori school, and we'd have pot luck days. One time, a mom brought homemade baked macaroni and cheese. My mind was blown . . . and so were my insides. Shortly after, I learned that all my stomach aches were from dairy. Years later, I decided I and my kids just couldn't live without mac and cheese, so I found a way to make it gluten free and dairy free . . . and just as delicious.

Cook the pasta according to the package instructions. Drain when done, don't rinse. Seriously, DO NOT RINSE.

Place the pasta in a bowl and drizzle with a little truffle, olive or avocado oil if you want a little extra finesse.

Place all sauce ingredients in a high powered blender or food processor and process until smooth.

Pour sauce over pasta and gently stir to mix together. You can totes stop and eat it like this, especially if you left the blender running and the sauce got hot. But, we're baking this Mac-N-Cheese so if you can wait, it's worth it. The sauce can also be poured over zoodles for a raw vegan Mac-N-Cheese like I served at my restaurant!

If you're going all in and want to make it even mo' gouda-ish (who doesn't?), mix in your extra cheeses (cheddar, gouda and cream) now and stir to combine well.

Dump it all into a baking dish. If you like extra crunch on top, cover with a layer of parmesan and then bake for 5-10 minutes or until it's as crispy and brown as you like.

Serve and enjoy! It should keep in the fridge for 3-5 days if it's sealed in an airtight container. We've NEVER had leftovers of this, though. You probably won't either.

VALT

vacon (pg. 24)

12 leaves bibb or boston lettuce (any will do, but these are perfect and buttery)

6 medium thick slices heirloom or any large tomato

1 large avocado, pitted and smashed

12 slices of yummy bread

CHIPOTLE MAYO

2 cups raw cashews (You can substitute macadamia nuts or pine nuts.)

¾ cup water

¼ cup oil (avocado, olive, or your favorite)

3 tablespoons lemon juice

2 tablespoons apple cider vinegar

1 tablespoon maple syrup (optional)

2 teaspoons chipotle powder

¼ teaspoon sea salt

1 pinch of cayenne pepper

MAKES: 6
PREP TIME: 50 MINS | COOK TIME: 20-30 MINS | TOTAL TIME: 1 HRS 20 MINS

Imagine if avocado toast and a BLT had a baby. That's what a VALT is. It's Vacon Avocado Lettuce and Tomato nestled between two toasty pieces of bread. Slather on some chipotle mayo and you have a sammie that's perfect for any time of day or night.

_____

Pat the zucchini and/or eggplant strips dry with a towel.

Place all the vacon ingredients in a container to marinate. Glass dishes, like Pyrex, are more eco friendly, but a plastic bag with the air pressed out of it really maximizes the flavor. Make sure to completely cover all the soon-to-be vacon strips in the marinade and let them sit for 30 minutes. Any longer than that and they'll become mushy.

In a large skillet over medium-high heat, add 1 teaspoon of oil and fry each vacon strip until they start to crisp. About 1-2 minutes per side.

Transfer each fried slice to a paper towel-lined plate to cool and drain excess oil.

For the mayo: put all ingredients in a high powered blender, and blend until smooth. This mayo can be stored in an airtight container in your refrigerator for up to seven days.

To assemble, start by toasting the bread slices.

Slather 6 of the slices of toast with 1 teaspoon chipotle mayo.

Next, layer a piece of lettuce on top of the mayo, and then top that with a slice of tomato and 2 or 3 pieces of vacon.

Smother top toast slice in smashed avocado, and place top slice (avocado side down) on top of sandwich.

Cut each sandwich in half from corner to corner. It makes the sandwich look larger and more appetizing. Plus it feels easier to eat. Enjoy!

PASTA BOLOGNESE

2 boxes of your favorite gluten-free pasta

2 heirloom tomatoes

1 pint mushrooms (I like baby bello and crimini best)

1 cup sun-dried tomatoes, soaked in warm water at least minutes to soften

1 cup parmesan (if you don't have parm on hand, simply throw in ½ cup nuts/seeds. I like Brazil nuts best, pumpkin seeds are solid, walnuts do great, an extra 1 tsp garlic powder and extra 1 tsp sea salt, plus 1 TB nutritional flakes)

½ cup fresh basil

½ cup olive oil

1 tablespoon dried oregano

1 tablespoon garlic powder

1 teaspoon onion powder

1 teaspoon sage powder

1 teaspoon cumin powder

½ teaspoon white pepper

½ teaspoon sea salt

SERVES: 4-6
PREP TIME: 10 MINS | COOK TIME: 15 MINS | TOTAL TIME: 25 MINS

Unlike most Pasta Bolognese recipes, this one is crazy simple (trust me), easy to whip together, and it's always been a crowd pleaser with my boys. And the fact that it's crammed full of nutrients and goodness is icing on the cake.

Submerge your tomatoes in a pan of hot water. The water should not be boiling. It should be more like an #instaworthy self-care Sunday hot bath temperature, with a teeny bit of steam. Let them soak for 5-10 minutes and then remove. Peel the skins from the tomatoes. They should slip off easily now. Next, quarter and deseed them with a sharp knife.

Cook pasta according to box directions. Pro tip: add a pinch of sea salt to the boiling water first and the water will boil faster. Seriously. That's science saying that, not me.

Put ALL the other ingredients in your food processor and pulse until it forms a crumbly thick sauce that looks like bolognese.

When your pasta is cooked, drain and return it to the pan. Drizzle a little olive oil over it and then add the sauce to the pasta. Keep the pan over low heat to warm everything through and bring the flavors together.

Plate and serve.

TATER TOTS

1 oversized cup grated zucchini (*peel the green skin first*)

1 rounded cup grated sweet potato

¼ cup finely chopped shallot or yellow onion

1 tablespoon nutritional flakes

1 tablespoon flaxseed or chia seed (*whole or ground*)

¼ cup water

1 teaspoon dried Italian seasoning

¼ teaspoon garlic powder

¼ teaspoon Himalayan salt

MARINARA

½ cup sundried tomato, soaked, rinsed, and drained

2 tablespoons olive oil + more to oil tater tots

2 tablespoons basil, chopped, packed

SERVES: 4-6 (DEPENDING ON THE SIZE OF THE TUMMIES)
PREP TIME: 15 MINS | COOK TIME: 20 MINS | TOTAL TIME: 35 MINS

The boys love helping out with these. It's also great life skills training in general, and a big part of preschool Montessori learning. Make sure to supervise any child helpers when they're peeling, cutting and grating. Kids especially love squishing them into little tots. Why not? Their hands are perfectly sized for it. If your kids are picky and freak at the sight of zucchini or sweet potato, you can totes swap them out for white potato. But I highly recommend giving this recipe a go as is.

Preheat oven to 400°F.

For the tots: mix 1 tablespoon of chia seeds or flaxseed with ¼ cup water. Stir well to combine, and let sit for at 5-10 minutes to thicken up. Set aside.

Place the grated zucchini and sweet potato in a clean dish towel (or, if you have it, a cheesecloth) and wring all of the excess water out.

Place the grated zucchini/sweet potato in a bowl along with all of the other ingredients except the olive oil, sundried tomato, dates and basil. Mix until combined.

Line a baking sheet with parchment paper. Take a tablespoon of the mixture and form it into a cylinder shape (enlist the help of small hands if you have any around). Repeat with the rest of the mixture. Arrange the tots (the taters, not the kiddos) on a single layer on the baking sheet and spray or brush the tops lightly with olive oil.

Bake about 10 minutes and then remove from oven. Using a spatula, flip the tots, top lightly with more olive oil, and then return to the oven. You can also lightly shake the tray to turn the tots. Bake another 10 minutes or until fluffy and cooked through.

For the marinara: purée sun dried tomatoes, olive oil, and basil in a food processor until smooth.

TIP:

You can make these ahead of time in batches and freeze. We've tossed frozen tots in an air fryer with great success, but the fresh don't hold up quite as well in the air fryer.

PIZZA DOUGH

1 cup almond flour

1 cup cassava flour (*You can substitute cauliflower flour.*)

¼ cup fine ground flaxseed meal

½ cup arrowroot starch

1 teaspoon cream of tartar

½ teaspoon baking soda

½ teaspoon garlic granules/powder

1 teaspoon pizza seasoning (*salt free*)

¾ cup water

¼ cup apple cider vinegar

½ cup olive oil

SERVES: 4-6
PREP TIME: 15 MINS | COOK TIME: 20 MINS | TOTAL TIME: 35 MINS

Looking for the perfectly thin and crispy crust with just the right amount of chew? This is the recipe you've been looking for. It's also an excellent way to get kids and friends in the kitchen. Host a Make Your Own Pizza dinner party and let everyone mix their own dough and get creative with the toppings. Happiness can come from an oven, and this recipe proves it.

Preheat oven to 400°F.

Mix all dry ingredients together in a bowl.

Mix wet ingredients together in a separate bowl.

Add wet ingredients to dry ingredients and mix well to completely incorporate them.

Divide dough into 2 rounds and shape into pizzas. We usually make ovals so it fits on a baking sheet more easily.

Bake for 5 minutes, remove, let cool, top with desired toppings and continue to cook for 10-15 minutes.

EASY OLIVE ROSEMARY GARLIC BREAD/ROLLS

1 box artisan bread mix (*I adore Simple Mills, but any gluten-free mix will do*)

1 8 ounce tub of plant-based cream cheese (*homemade or store bought - Kite Hill is great*)

2 tablespoons olive oil

2 tablespoons egg replacer (*Bob's Redmill Gluten-Free*)

¾ cup water

¼ cup apple cider vinegar

ADD INS

¼ cup sliced olives (*anything from Kalamata and Castelvetrano to canned black olives taste great!*)

3 tablespoons fresh or dried rosemary

3 tablespoons minced garlic

¼ cup sundried tomatoes

SERVES: 6-12
ACTIVE TIME: 5 MINS | BAKE TIME: 30 MINS | TOTAL TIME: 35 MINS

Preheat oven to 350°F.

Combine all ingredients in a large bowl and mix well.

Spray a muffin pan with oil or use muffin liners, and then roll the dough into balls and drop into muffin tin. You can also spread the dough out on a cookie sheet for "flat bread" or bake it in a loaf pan for bread you can slice up and serve.

Bake for 30 minutes and enjoy!

FLAX CRACKERS

2 cups gold flaxseed

2 cups brown flaxseed

2 cups zucchini, peeled and chopped

4 cloves garlic

2 tablespoons onion powder

2 tablespoons garlic powder

2 tablespoons sea salt

Optional: 1 teaspoon chili powder. Try chipotle powder for a smoky flavor, or cayenne for extra spice!

SERVES: 4-6
PREP TIME: 1 HR 15 MINS | COOK TIME: 1 HRS | TOTAL TIME: 2 HRS 15 MINS

Preheat oven on the lowest setting.

Soak flaxseeds in enough water to cover (about 2 cups) in a mixing bowl, for 1 hour.

Blend remaining ingredients in a high powered blender or food processor until smooth.

Combine blended mix with soaked flaxseed mix. Refrigerate 30 minutes (makes it easier to spread).

Line a baking tray with lightly oiled parchment paper. This makes it easier to lift crackers off later.

Use an offset spatula to spread the mix on the baking trays in a thin, even layer-- about 1/8-1/4" depending how thick you like your crackers. They will shrink a little.

Bake on lowest setting for 1 hour. After 1 hour, check to see if they are dry to the touch. If they are, remove from the oven. If they are still wet to the touch, keep baking until they are.

Once removed from the oven, carefully lift the parchment paper/cracker spread out of the baking tray and set aside. Next, add a new piece of lightly oiled parchment paper to the tray and then flip the tray upside-down on top of the crackers. Next, grab the bottom parchment paper (the one with the baked crackers on it) and carefully flip it over so that the tray is upright. What we're doing is flipping the crackers over so we can bake the bottom.

Once the tray is flipped, peel off the original parchment paper. If you want to shape the crackers before doing the second bake, I recommend using a pizza cutter to cut straight lines, or a cookie cutter if you prefer rounds or other fun shapes.

Return the tray to the oven for another hour or until the crackers are bone dry.

Remove from the oven and let crackers cool until you can touch them. Once cooled, break into desired cracker sizes. These will keep in an airtight container for 2 weeks.

VEGGIES

LEMON CARROTS WITH GREENS PESTO

1 bunch carrots

¼ cup olive oil

1 lemon, juiced (about ¼ cup lemon juice)

1 tablespoon finely chopped parsley

½ teaspoon sea salt

CARROT GREENS

1 bunch of carrot top greens

½ cup pumpkin seeds

½ cup olive oil

½ teaspoon garlic powder

½ teaspoon sea salt

1 tablespoon nutritional flakes (optional)

SERVES: 2-4
PREP TIME: 5 MINS | COOK TIME: 30 MINS | TOTAL TIME: 35 MINS

If you like something with a bit more "bite" go with arugula, parsley, cilantro, microgreens (they have a bitter punch), dandelion greens, chard, kale, endive and even romaine lettuce. If softer, smoother flavors are more your speed go with spinach, basil, and butter lettuce. Looking for a seed or nut alternative? Try pine nuts, pistachios, walnuts, almonds, brazil nuts, cashews, or sunflower seeds

Preheat oven to 450 F.

Cut the carrots in half lengthwise, place on a parchment paper-lined cookie sheet or baking pan (cookie sheets don't have sides, baking pans do!), and then drizzle with olive oil and lemon juice. Finally, sprinkle with parsley and sea salt.

Roast for 30 minutes until done.

For the pesto: while the carrots are roasting, place all pesto ingredients in a food processor and pulse until you reach your desired smoothness. I like a little more texture to mine, but go with what makes you happy.

PERFECT POTATOES

4 pounds baby potatoes, washed

1 cup olive oil

2 cups lemon juice (*ideally fresh*)

1 teaspoon sea salt

Sea salt, to taste

Fresh ground black pepper, to taste

SERVES: 4-6
PREP TIME: 5 MINS | COOK TIME: 45 MINS | TOTAL TIME: 50 MINS

Of all the ways I love potatoes, I do dare say, the potatoes in this recipe are PERFECT--so much so, it's the name of the recipe. And, I would go even further and say I would be okay if this were the only way I could eat potatoes for the rest of my life. I'd mourn the tater tots and shoestring fries, but a bite of these and I would forget they even exist.

Preheat the oven to 400 F.

In a large pot over high heat, bring the potatoes, 1 teaspoon sea salt and water to cover the potatoes to a boil. Boil until soft, about 15-20 minutes.

Turn off the heat and, using a slotted spoon, transfer potatoes to a large baking dish.

Cut the potatoes in half or leave whole. Your call. They're delicious both ways.

Drizzle with olive oil.

Douse in lemon juice.

Season with sea salt and pepper to taste.

Return the baking dish to the oven and bake for 25 minutes or until the desired crispy exterior level is reached.

MAPLE ROASTED VEGGIES

2 delicata squashes, de-seeded and cut in half moon slices

2 acorn squashes, de-seeded and cut in thick strips

2 fennel bulbs, sliced in rings (*like onions*)

1 pound baby carrots

1 pound broccoli florets

¼ cup olive oil

¼ cup maple syrup

⅛ teaspoon cinnamon

⅛ teaspoon cardamon

⅛ teaspoon paprika

⅛ teaspoon cumin

⅛ teaspoon sea salt

SERVES: 4-6
PREP TIME: 10 MINS | COOK TIME: 45 MINS | TOTAL TIME: 55 MINS

These came about as a sort of happy accident turned super success. I had an impromptu dinner party and no time to shop. It was Fall so I took the squash that was the centerpiece and fluffed up the menu. It was the highlight of the evening. Everyone wanted the recipe and it's been requested at several dinners every since.

———————

Preheat the oven to 400 F.

Evenly spread delicata squash, acorn squash, fennel rings, baby carrots and broccoli florets out on a parchment paper-lined baking sheet.

In a small bowl, whisk together olive oil, maple syrup and all the spices.

Drizzle the maple oil mix over the veggies.

Bake in the oven for 45 minutes, or until the veggies are tender and the edges begin to caramelize.

SPICE IT UP:
Add 1 tablespoon of harissa paste, sriracha, hatch chili paste or even pureed kimchi to the maple/oil/spice mix.

MEDITERRANEAN VEGGIES

4 medium portobello mushroom caps, whole (or 12 whole baby portobello mushrooms)

1 large eggplant, sliced in rounds

2 large zucchinis, sliced lengthwise

2 red bell peppers, sliced in half, de-stemmed and de-seeded

2 yellow bell peppers, sliced in half, de-stemmed and de-seeded

2 orange bell peppers, sliced in half, de-stemmed and de-seeded

2 medium to large vine ripened tomatoes, de-stemmed and cut in half across the middle width

¼ cup olive oil

¼ cup balsamic vinegar

Sea salt, to taste

Fresh ground black pepper, to taste

GARNISH

Fresh flat leaf parsley leaves, chopped

Fresh oregano

Balsamic vinegar, to drizzle

Olive oil, to drizzle

SERVES: 4-6
PREP TIME: 10 MINS | COOK TIME: 30-40 MINS | TOTAL TIME: 40-50 MINS

These can be done on the grill, but this recipe is for the oven. It's easy to prep, then set it and forget it.

Preheat the oven to 400 F.

Spread the veggies evenly on a baking sheet.

Drizzle with olive oil and balsamic vinegar.

Sprinkle with sea salt and pepper.

Bake in the oven for 30-40 minutes or until they reach your desired level of roastiness.

To serve, drizzle with more balsamic and olive oil, and sprinkle with fresh parsley and oregano. Finish it off with more sea salt and cracked pepper, if desired.

SAUCE, DRESS, DIP, AND TOP

CHIMICHURRI

1 bunch parsley (*about 1 cup, packed*)

½ bunch cilantro (*about ½ cup, packed*)

4 cloves garlic

2 teaspoons dried oregano

½ cup olive oil

1 tablespoon apple cider vinegar

1 tablespoon lemon juice

½ teaspoon sea salt

½ teaspoon red pepper flakes

Black pepper to taste

Optional: fortified nutritional flakes, to taste

SERVES: 4
TOTAL TIME: 5 MINS

Aside from being fun to say--chimichurri, chimichurri, chimichurri--this easy to make pesto-like sauce is packed with flavor and can be put on anything from carrots and potatoes to proteins. It also makes an amazing rub or marinade.

———————

Throw everything--yes, everything--in a food processor and pulse until the parsley and cilantro are chopped up into tiny pieces.

Store refrigerated in a sealed container for up to a week.

BEARNAISE

¼ cup white-wine vinegar

1 small shallot, peeled & minced

1 tablespoon + 1 teaspoon tarragon leaves, chopped

½ teaspoon fresh ground black pepper

¾ cups butter of choice, melted (*I'm obsessed with Miyokos European Style plant based butter*)

3 tablespoons nutritional yeast

3 tablespoons water

1 teeny tiny pinch Kala Namak black salt (*find online or at Indian grocers*)

Sea salt to taste

Squeeze of lemon

SERVES: 4-6
TOTAL TIME: 25 MINS

One of the five mother sauces in French cuisine, bearnaise is similar to hollandaise in that it's composed primarily of buttah and egg. This version is sans egg, obviously, and every bit as delish. Drizzle this on breakfast dishes, steamed or grilled veggies, potatoes or dip and lick your fingers in it a lá my kids.

In a small saucepan over medium heat, bring the vinegar, shallots, 1 tablespoon of tarragon, and black pepper to a boil. Reduce heat and simmer until liquid is reduced to a third, about 5 minutes.

Remove from heat, set aside to cool.

In a blender, add cooled shallot/tarragon mix, nutritional yeast, kala namak salt and water. Pulse to combine.

Turn the blender on low and slowly add in the melted butter, about a tablespoon at a time until everything begins to emulsify and thicken. Once everything has fully incorporated and thickened, add sea salt to taste, and a quick squeeze of fresh lemon juice.

If the sauce is too thick, you can stir in a splash of warm water.

Add in the last teaspoon of tarragon and serve.

BECHAMEL

4 tablespoons of buttah

8 ounces milk of choice (I like unsweetened, plain almond for this)

½ cup flour of choice (I like cassava flour, or an equal flour replacement GF blend)

Whole black peppercorns

2 sprigs flat leaf parsley

1 medium shallot, peeled and cut in half

1 large bay leaf

Sea salt, to taste

White pepper, to taste

MAKES: ABOUT 1 ½ - 2 CUPS
TOTAL TIME: 15-20 MINS

AKA "white sauce" this creamy smooth sauce is one of the French "mother sauces" - although it originated in Italy, where it's Besciamella. It's most basic version is just butter, milk, flour and salt & pepper - but I like more depth in all my flavors, so no exceptions were made here. It's still quick and easy and I can be easily upgraded to a white mac n cheese sauce by adding a sharp (white) cheddar or gruyere - or both!

Heat a saucepan over low heat on the stove top. Plop in the buttah to melt it. Once just melted, add in the flour and gently whisk smooth, being careful not to let the buttah turn brown.

In a separate pot, over low/medium heat (on a scale of 1 being the lowest and 10 being the highest heat, you want a 3), add in the milk, shallot, bay leaf, parsley and whole black peppercorns, stirring often - about 2-3 minutes, do not let it bubble or overheat.

Remove the milk from the heat, and pour through a sieve (or just scoop out everything but the milk).

Slowly pour the milk mixture into the saucepan with the buttah and flour (fancy term: "roux" pronounced like kangaroo, without the kanga), and gently whisk to incorporate.

Add salt and pepper to taste.

Cook, stirring often, for 10 minutes until smooth.

BEURRE BLANC

¼ cup dry white wine (*try a Muscadet*)

¼ cup white wine vinegar

2 tablespoons shallots, peeled & chopped

⅓ cup heavy cream (*I like half coconut & half almond*)

¼ teaspoon sea salt

⅛ teaspoon white pepper

1 cup cold/hard butter of choice, cut into 1 TB size cubes

MAKES: ABOUT 2 CUPS
TOTAL TIME: 10-15 MINS

Literally: white butter. This velvety rich sauce is perfectly balanced with sweetness and tang thanks to the wine and vinegar that cut through the buttah's richness. This sauce is easier to make than a hollandaise. It's cooked in a single pot until it reduces down. No need to mess with a double boiler or eggs, which a hollandaise does.

In a medium saucepan over medium heat, bring the white wine, white wine vinegar and shallots to a boil. Let reduce down for about 3-5 minutes until there are just a few tablespoons worth of liquid in the pan.

Add cream, salt and pepper, and bring the heat up to a quick boil for a minute or so.

Reduce heat to lowest setting, add the butter a few cubes at a time, whisking non-stop as you go. Working quickly to not overheat, add in a few more butter cubes once melted, continue whisking, and repeat until all of the butter is in and the sauce begins to look smooth.

Remove from heat, and season with salt and pepper to taste.

Pour the sauce through a mesh sieve, into a serving dish, to strain out the shallot pieces. Serve immediately.

TARRAGON BUTTAH

1 cup softened butter

2 tablespoons fresh tarragon leaves

MAKES: 1 CUP
TOTAL TIME: 10-15 MINS

Don't freak at the description, but tarragon has a mellow anise (aka licorice) flavor, and it is absolutely beautiful when combined with buttah. The subtle complexity will enhance anything you smear it on.

_____

Gently roll the tarragon leaves between your palms to release the flavor.

Mix together with the butter until incorporated.

GARLIC BUTTAH

1 cup softened butter

2 cloves garlic, minced (*or 1 tsp garlic powder*)

MAKES: 1 CUP
TOTAL TIME: 10-15 MINS

_____

Mix the ingredients together in a bowl until smooth and incorporated. That's it.

Fancy it up with optional add-ins like 1 teaspoon of Italian seasoning and/or ¼ cup parmesan, or a squeeze of fresh lemon juice, for some zing. I generally serve this softened, but you can put it into a silicone mold to shape it, and then plop it out when ready to use.

SAUCE TOMAT

4 large heirloom or beefsteak tomatoes

4 tablespoons butter of choice

2 cloves garlic, minced

Sea salt, to taste

Fresh ground pepper, to taste

SERVES: 2-4
PREP TIME: 10 MINS | COOK TIME: 20-30 MINS | TOTAL TIME: 30-40 MINS

Fill a large pot with water and bring to a boil.

While water is heating up, cut an X in the bottom of each tomato, and then cut the core out of the tops of the tomatoes. You're going to peel them in a bit, and this step will make it so much easier.

Reduce water to a simmer, and add the tomatoes, cooking for 1 minute. When the skin around the "X" that you cut looks loose, remove the tomatoes using tongs or a spoon please. Run the tomatoes under cold water to keep them from cooking more. We just want the skin to slip off easily. This is just the prep to cook.

Cut the tomatoes into quarters along the "X" that marks the spot and peel the skin off. Then scoop the seeds out over a mesh strainer set on a bowl (to catch the tomato juice - don't throw it away), then dice the tomatoes.

Heat the butter in a large pan over low heat. When the butter has melted, add in the garlic and bring the heat up to medium to gently caramelize the garlic.

Add in the tomatoes, and season with sea salt and pepper. Stir occasionally.

When tomatoes start to break down, add tomato juice, reduce heat to low and cook, stirring occasionally, until excess liquid is gone.

Serve over your favorite pasta or dip all your favorite bready items in it.

VINAIGRETTE

3 tablespoons shallots, peeled and minced

¼ cup white wine vinegar

¾ cup olive oil

2 teaspoon dijon mustard

¼ teaspoon sea salt (*or to taste*)

Fresh ground pepper, to taste

OPTIONAL ADD-INS

Fresh herbs (*I love thyme.*)

Honey/maple syrup/fruit syrup

MAKES: 10 OUNCES
TOTAL TIME: 5 MINS

The only vinaigrette recipe you'll ever need. Quick and easy to make, but bursting with flavor.

_____

Place all ingredients in a mason jar, put the lid on it and shake vigorously.

OR if you would rather skip the man power - put it all in a blender and give it a few quick pulses. You can also use an immersion blender if you have one.

PARMESAN

1 cup Brazil nuts (*or substitutes*)

¼ cup nutritional yeast

1 ½ teaspoons garlic powder

½ teaspoon sea salt, to taste

MAKES: 1¼ CUPS
TOTAL TIME: 3 MINS

Quick and easy to make, loaded with nutrients, and it can be sprinkled on or mixed into basically anything. My go-to "base" for this is Brazil nuts, but you can substitute blanched almonds, walnuts, pinenuts, cashews, or macadamia nuts instead.

Pulse all ingredients in a food processor until small and crumbly parmesan like texture.

Use just like traditional parmesan cheese and add to your favorite dishes. Keep refrigerated for up to one week.

BASIL PESTO

1 cup basil leaves, packed

½ cup olive oil

1 tablespoon pine nuts

2 cloves garlic

¼ cup Parmesan (*pg. 115*)

Sea salt, to taste

Fresh ground pepper, to taste

SERVES: 4
TOTAL TIME: 10 MINS

Basic, but never boring. Spread this basil pesto on bread, toss it with pasta, layer in a sandwich, add some pizzazz to your avocado toast, or eat it straight up as a dip. You cannot go wrong with this one.

———————

Place all ingredients in a food processor and puree for 3-5 minutes. Smear on everything from pizza to avocado toast to pasta, or eat it with a spoon. It's that good.

Get creative:

Substitute other nuts/seeds for the pine nuts, or try other greens.

SOME OF OUR PERSONAL FAMILY FAVORITES:

Carrot greens with pepitos (pumpkin seeds)

Arugula with pistachios

Kale with walnuts

Parsley with macadamia nuts

Spinach with pistachios & some Feta (love VioLife)

MARINARA

¼ cup olive oil

1 small onion, minced

5 cloves garlic, minced

3 sprigs fresh basil

2 28-ounce cans whole, peeled tomatoes (*or use the sauce tomat recipe on pg. 113*)

Sea salt, to taste

Fresh ground pepper, to taste

SERVES: 2-4
PREP TIME: 5 MINS | COOK TIME: 25-30 MINS | TOTAL TIME: 30-35 MINS

There are so many great store bought options, but none ever match the quality of freshly home-made marinara. Running short on time? Use the sauce tomat recipe as a base (pg. 113), or you can make it quicker using canned tomatoes. Delicious both ways.

_____

Sauté the onion in the olive oil in a medium pot over medium heat for 8-10 minutes, stirring occasionally.

Add garlic and continue stirring until soft, about 5 minutes.

Roll the basil briefly between your palms to release its oils and then add to the pot.

Add the tomatoes and crush them with the back of a large wooden spoon. Or, dump in your sauce tomát to be totes from scratch and feel fancy saying you used a sauce tomát base. Ooh la la.

Season with salt and pepper to taste.

Bring the sauce to a simmer and reduce heat.

Continue to simmer, stirring occasionally, until the sauce thickens. About 1 hour.

Add more salt and pepper to taste.

BBQ SAUCE

24 ounce canned diced
tomatoes, strained

6 ounce tomato paste

½ cup apple cider vinegar

⅓ cup blackstrap molasses

¼ cup coconut aminos

2 tablespoons olive oil

1 ½ tablespoons garlic powder

1 ½ tablespoons chili powder

1 ½ tablespoons smoked
paprika powder

1 tablespoon onion powder

1 tablespoon liquid smoke
(*optional*)

1 teaspoon sea salt

1 teaspoon black pepper

MAKES: 4 CUPS
PREP TIME: 5 MINS | COOK TIME: 10-15 MINS | TOTAL TIME: 15-20 MINS

Being a Texan, BBQ sauce is a big deal. It has to be PERFECT. No worries, I've got you. While this recipe IS perfect without modification, no matter your mood, there's a variation for you.

Place all ingredients in a food processor and puree for 3-5 minutes until smooth.

Pour the sauce into a medium sized saucepan and bring to a simmer. Let simmer on low, stirring occasionally, until sauce thickens. About 5-10 minutes. You can skip the cooking, but that's how the flavors infuse, so don't.

MIX IT UP:

SPICY - double the chili powder and pepper

SWEET - swap out molasses for honey and only use ½ tablespoon chili powder and ½ tablespoon of regular paprika

TANGY - double up the apple cider vinegar

MAYO

2 cups raw unsalted cashews

½ cup warm water

¼ cup oil (I use avocado or olive)

3 tablespoons fresh lemon juice

2 tablespoons apple cider vinegar

1 teaspoon yellow mustard

¼ teaspoon sea salt

MAKES: 3 CUPS
TOTAL TIME: 5 MINS

What do you call a laughing jar of mayonnaise? LMAyO. Seriously though, this stuff is legit, and for your tastebud's optimal pleasure, I've included a few variations to mix it up if your adventurous.

———————

Place all ingredients in a food processor and puree smooth for 3-5 minutes. That's it. Easy peasy, lemon squeezy.

Dish it on anything you would traditionally put mayo on, or use it as a dip.

Keep refrigerated in a sealed container for up to a week.

NEW TWIST:

CHIPOTLE - add in 1 tsp chipotle pepper, ½ tsp paprika and a dash of cayenne

GARLIC - add in 2 cloves garlic, minced

DIJONAISSE - add in 1 ½ TB dijon or spicy brown mustard

AVOCADO CREAM

2 large avocados

1 tablespoon milk of choice (*I use almond*)

½ lime, juiced

½ teaspoon garlic powder

Sea salt, to taste

MAKES: 1 CUP
TOTAL TIME: 5 MINS

What do you call young avocados? Avokiddos!

———————————

Place all ingredients in a food processor, and puree until smooth and creamy. If too thick, add a bit more milk until desired consistency is reached. That's it. Pretty easy, but you can upcharge your family $2.

PAN SAUCE

1 tablespoon olive oil

1 shallot, minced

1 clove garlic, minced

¼ cup wine (red or white)

¾ cup veggie stock

2 tablespoons butter of choice (I love Miyokos plant based)

Optional: 1 teaspoon starch (I use arrowroot) mixed smooth with 1 tablespoon warm water

Sea salt, to taste

White pepper, to taste

SERVES: 2-4
PREP TIME: 3 MINS | COOK TIME: 12 MINS | TOTAL TIME: 15 MINS

Pan sauce can take any meal to the next level. Similar to a gravy in use, drizzle it on and gobble it down.

Sauté the garlic and shallot in olive oil over medium-high heat, about 2-3 minutes.

Add in the wine, bring to a simmer, then reduce heat to low. Simmer for 3 minutes, scraping bottom of pan, until liquid reduces to half.

Add in stock, stir and bring to a simmer again. Simmer 3-5 minutes until liquid reduces by half.

Add in the butter and stir in until completely melted.

For a thicker sauce, whisk in the starch/water mix (pre-mix so it does not clump). Let simmer for another 20-30 seconds to thicken.

For a thinner sauce: stir in a little more stock until desired consistency is reached.

TIPS:

Add in fresh sprigs of thyme to the pan with the garlic and shallot and stir in a squeeze of lemon at the end. Substitute bourbon for wine. Toss sliced mushrooms (try Cremini or baby Portobellos) into the pan with the garlic and shallot.

CHOCOLATE SAUCE

⅔ cup coconut oil, melted

1 cup cacao powder

½ cup maple syrup

¼ teaspoon vanilla

Pinch of sea salt

MAKES: 1 CUP
TOTAL TIME: 5 MINS

It's dangerous just how easy this sauce is to make. But indulge away, you deserve it. Plus, it's health food.

———————————

Blend all ingredients together in a high powered blender, until smooth.

Put it on everything. Literally, everything. Enjoy.

Keep in a sealed container, refrigerated, for up to a week.

COCONUT CREAM

¾ cup coconut cream

¼ cup maple syrup or honey

¼ teaspoon vanilla

Pinch of sea salt

MAKES: 1 CUP
TOTAL TIME: 5 MINS

Anything goes with this: drizzle on cakes, dunk fruit in it, or add it to your morning beverage. It's all good.

———————————

Blend all ingredients together in a high powered blender, until smooth.

Keep in a sealed container, refrigerated, for up to one week.

CASHEW CREAM

1 cup cashews

1 ½ cups hot water

¼ cup maple syrup or honey

¼ teaspoon vanilla

Pinch of sea salt

MAKES: 1 CUP
PREP TIME: 5 MINS | TOTAL TIME: 10 MINS

Sweet creamy goodness for your body and soul. You can also replace the cashews with raw unsalted Macadamia nuts. If you do, be sure to double the soaking time.

_____

Soak the cashews in the hot water for 5 minutes to soften.

Drain water from cashews, and dump all ingredients in a high powered blender and blend smooth.

Keep in a sealed container for up to one week.

PARTY FOOD

SPICY NUTS

½ cup almonds

½ cup pistachios (*shelled*)

½ cup macadamia nuts

½ cup walnuts

½ cup pumpkin seeds

½ cup Brazil nuts

¼ cup oil (*I use olive or avocado*)

2 teaspoons garlic powder

2 teaspoons smoked paprika

1 teaspoon cumin

1 teaspoon coriander

1 teaspoon cayenne

½ teaspoon cinnamon

¼ teaspoon mustard powder

¼ teaspoon ginger powder

¼ teaspoon sea salt

MAKES: 3 CUPS
PREP TIME: 5 MINS | COOK TIME: 10 MINS | COOL TIME: 5 MINS | TOTAL TIME: 15-20 MINS

We are nuts about nuts in my house. There's always a bowl of mixed nuts out, and I refill it every day. It LOOKS like the same bowl always sitting there, but it's not. These spicy nuts are always in the bowl rotation, especially around the holidays. Guests ask all the time where I bought the awesome mix. Plus, it makes your house smell amazing when cooking.

Preheat the oven to 400 F.

Place all of the nuts and seeds in a large bowl, set aside.

In a smaller bowl, mix together the oil and seasonings, whisk to fully incorporate. Then pour the oil mixture over the nuts and seeds, and toss to fully coat.

Bake in the oven for 5 minutes, and then remove, toss, and spread them back out evenly. Return them to the oven for 5 more minutes.

After the final 5 minutes, remove them from the oven and let cool completely before tasting. They will be super hot (not spicy hot). Be warned: they will burn you. That's experience speaking, folks.

GUACAMOLE

4 medium ripe avocados

1 lime, peeled (*you read that right*)

1 bunch fresh cilantro, chopped (*about 1 cup, stems and all*)

1 jalapeño pepper (*de-seeded for mild flavor, or 2 jalapeños for spicier*)

1 Serrano pepper (*de-seeded for mild flavor, or 2 jalapeños for spicier*)

1 sprig of green onion (*this isn't traditional, but adds amazing depth and it's own baby kick*)

1 clove garlic

½ teaspoon sea salt

MAKES: 1 ½ TO 2 CUPS
TOTAL TIME: 5 MINS

Repeat after me: tomatoes do not belong in guacamole. Neither do onion chunks. Neither does any sort of dairy. I promise. It's a scam by restaurants to add cheap filler. Speaking of which, most restaurants make their guac in massive batches in advance, then scoop off the darkened top that was exposed to the air before serving. If you ask for no salt, they'll have to make it fresh (cross your fingers they have avocados on hand). I've made my own guac many times at the table. Just ask the server for avocado, cilantro, lime, and chopped jalapenos and/or serranos.

——————

If you have a molcajete, congratulations, you're awesome. You'll want to hand chop all the ingredients to make it easier to smash together. Then smash away.

If elbow grease isn't your thing, put all ingredients in a food processor and pulse/process to desired consistency.

MOTHER LOVIN' SALSA

3 medium tomatoes, de-stemmed

½ cup cilantro, packed

3 cloves garlic

1 jalapeño pepper (de-seed for more mild flavor)

1 Serrano pepper (de-seed if you don't like spice!)

1 lime, peeled (yep, peeled, just cut the peel off)

1 tablespoon fortified nutritional flakes (optional add in, gives it more depth, umami and vitamins!)

1 habanero pepper (optional, if you really like spice)

MAKES: 2 CUPS
TOTAL TIME: 5 MINS

My salsa brings all the boys to the yard… or kitchen… or wherever it is. I can't even count the number of parties i've been invited to - not hosting - where the host asked me to bring this salsa. With pleasure, I'm guaranteed to get to consume delicious and spicy salsa!

_____

Put all ingredients in a food processor and pulse to desired consistency.

Keeps in the fridge in an airtight container for 3 days, after that it starts to ferment. I have 100% eaten fermented salsa. It has probiotic benefits, but you consume it at your own risk. Ok? Got that?

CALIENTE QUESO BLANCO

1 cup cashews (*raw, unsalted*)

¼ cup warm water

1 teaspoon sea salt

1 ½ tablespoon lemon juice

4 tablespoons Nutritional flakes

1 ½ teaspoons garlic powder

1 ½ teaspoons onion powder

1 tablespoon apple cider vinegar

½ cup diced tomatoes

1 fresh jalapeno pepper, diced/chopped

2 tablespoons pickled jalapenos

2 tablespoons pickled jalapeno juice

SERVES: 4 -6
TOTAL TIME: 5-10 MINS

Queso that won't leave you bloated or running for the toilet. Bonus: so simple kids can make it. Seriously, my two older boys made the queso in this photo. I can take credit for the plating and tasting.

_____

Puree cashews and water together in a food processor until smooth.

Add in sea salt, lemon juice, nutritional flakes, garlic powder, onion powder and apple cider vinegar. Process to combine until smooth.

Add in the diced tomatoes, jalapenos and jalapeno juice. Pulse briefly to incorporate.

It can be eaten cold. If you prefer it warm, pour the queso into a pan on the stovetop over low heat, stirring occasionally to heat evenly.

Heat to warm thoroughly, about 5 minutes. Serve with tortilla chips or veggies, or pour over tacos.

BUFFALLO WINGS + RANCH

MARINADE MIXTURE

1 large bulb garlic, peeled

1 red bell pepper, seeded and chopped

1 stalk celery, roughly chopped

2 green onions/scallions

½ cup your fave BBQ sauce (*aka my recipe, pg.123*)

½ cup olive oil

½ cup apple cider vinegar

¼ cup flat leaf parsley

1 tablespoon molasses

1 tablespoon red hot sauce (*like Tabasco or sriracha*)

SPICE MIXTURE

3 tablespoons paprika (*smoked, spanish or regular*)

1 tablespoon sea salt

1 tablespoon onion powder

½ tablespoon Italian seasoning

½ tablespoon garlic powder

½ tablespoon dried oregano

½ tablespoon dried thyme

½ tablespoon black pepper

½ tablespoon white pepper

½ tablespoon cayenne pepper

WINGS

½ cup apple cider vinegar

3 heads cauliflower, cut into florets

SERVES: 4 TO 6
PREP TIME: 10 MINS | COOK TIME: 20-30 MINS | MARINADE TIME: 1 HOUR+
TOTAL TIME: 1 HOUR 30-40 MIN+ (DEPENDS ON MARINATING TIME)

Why is spicy the only flavor our butts can taste? On another note... I dare you to try these spicy creole style buffalo wings, and let me know what you think on IG.

Disclaimer: it's not buffalo at all, and in no way related to the sauces out of Buffalo NY. This is way spicier. Trust me. They're not wings either. So basically tjos whole recipe name is a lie. But it's delicious.

_____

Preheat the oven to 450F.

Line 2 baking sheets with parchment paper

Place cauliflower florets in a large mixing bowl. You may need to do this in batches. Toss with apple cider vinegar to coat (could use a massive plastic bag too).

Mix all spice mix ingredients together.

Mix spice mixture and cauliflower in zip-top bag(s) and toss until coated. Let sit while you make the sauce.

In a food processor or blender, blend all marinade ingredients until smooth.

Pour marinade ingredients over cauliflower and marinate for at least one hour, or overnight.

Arrange the cauliflower on a single layer on the prepared baking sheets, making sure florets do not touch one another. Bake for 20-25 minutes until crisp on the edges.

Remove from heat, let stand for 3-5 minutes to crisp more. Transfer to plate(s) to serve.

JESSICA'S INFAMOUS MARGARITA

2 Serrano or Jalapeno peppers, sliced lengthwise

1 bunch of cilantro

1 cup tequila

1 cup fresh squeezed lime juice

½ cup orange liquor (*I like Cointreau*)

½ cup fresh squeezed orange juice

RIM

1 teaspoon chili powder

1 teaspoon smoked salt

¼ teaspoon paprika

GARNISH

Lime wedges or circles

Jalapeno and/or Serrano slices

SERVES: 2-4
PREP TIME: 5 MINS | SET TIME: 6 HRS | TOTAL TIME: 6 HRS 5 MINS

Take your margarita game up a few notches with this recipe. It's become the "signature house drink" at my home - by far the most requested when guests over 21 stop by.

———————

Mix together all the margarita ingredients. Let sit in the fridge for 6 hours, or overnight.

Mix together all of the rim ingredients. Put the rim mix on a plate, rub a lime wedge around the rim of a glass, and then turn the glass upside down on the plate and wiggle it in the spicy salt mix to coat the rim.

Fill rimmed glass with ice and margarita mix, garnish with lime wedge and spicy pepper slices.

Enjoy.

HOLIDAY CHEER

1 cup strong brewed french roast coffee, hot, but not Starbucks hot.

1 pint vanilla bean ice cream, slightly softened

1 cup damn good whiskey

1 cup white rum

RIM

1 teaspoon maple sugar

1 teaspoon dates

¼ teaspoon nutmeg

GARNISH

Nutmeg (*fresh is best, but any will do*)

SERVES: 2-5
TOTAL TIME: 6 MINS

This is not eggnog, but it is delicious and a huge hit at holiday parties.

_____

Mix together all of the eggnog ingredients. Stirring well to incorporate.

Mix together all of the rim ingredients. Put the rim mix on a plate, wet the rim of a glass, then turn the glass upside down on the plate and wiggle it in the rim mix to coat the rim.

Fill rimmed glass with ice and eggnog mix, garnish with a quick grind or dash of nutmeg.

Woohoo! I made it through without writing a single rim job joke. That's okay, you probably thought it. I sure did.

THE BLOODY BEST BLOODY

48 ounces low sodium tomato juice

3 tablespoons horseradish

3 tablespoons worcestershire sauce

3 teaspoons celery salt

2 teaspoons garlic salt

½ - 2 tablespoons Tabasco sauce (*to taste*)

Fresh ground black pepper

1 cup Vodka (*or swap for Tequila*)

RIM

1 tablespoon celery salt

1 tablespoon sea salt

⅛ - ¼ teaspoon chili powder

GARNISH
(*1 of each per glass*)

celery stalks, jarred pepperoncini peppers, lime wedges, lemon wedges, jalapeño stuffed olives, freshly ground pepper, drink sticks

SERVES: 4-6
TOTAL TIME: 5 MINS

The key to a good Bloody Mary is spice. The classic recipe is bland, which is probably why so many people are not fans of this delicious drink. Feeling feisty? Swap the vodka for tequila and you've got a Bloody Maria!

———————————

Mix together all of the Bloody Mary (or Maria) ingredients. Mix very well.

Mix together all of the rim ingredients. Put the rim mix on a plate, rub a lemon wedge around the rim of a glass, then turn the glass upside down on the plate and wiggle it in the spicy salt mix to coat the rim. You can use a lime to wet the rim for a Bloody Maria.

Fill the rimmed glass with ice and Bloody Mary mix, garnish with all the garnishes. More is more here.

#INSTAWORTHYAF

FRIED RICE

veggs (pg. 23)

½ cup buttah

1 pint mushrooms of choice
(I like the "chef's mix" found
prepackaged at some grocery
stores)

½ cup diced asparagus

½ cup diced carrots

¼ cup diced scallions

2 tablespoons Chinese Five
Spice Blend

1 pkg rice, cooked and cooled
(I love Right Rice, made
from lentils/chickpeas, but
cauliflower rice and regular
rice work great too)

SERVES: 4-6
PREP TIME: 10 MINS | COOK TIME: 20 MINS | TOTAL TIME: 30 MINS

Make veggs (recipe on pg. 23).

In a very large skillet over med-high heat, brown half the buttah.

Toss in the veggies and seasoning, stir while it fries.

Reduce heat to medium and add in the rest of the buttah. Cook until desired doneness. I like my shrooms crispy, so I tend to cook them longer (10-ish minutes).

Turn the heat off and toss the rice in. Mix everything to combine and then serve and enjoy.

SHROOM PAELLA

3 tablespoons oil (I recommend olive or avocado)

4 cloves garlic, minced

1 teaspoons red pepper flakes

2 cups rice (I used cauliflower rice)

½ cup onion, minced

½ teaspoon saffron threads (sometimes I go up to 1 teaspoons! So good!)

2 bay leaf

1 quart water

5 sprigs fresh thyme

3 ½ pounds mushrooms, sliced (I used shiitake, oyster, trumpet, and cremini)

1 red bell pepper, chopped

2 lemons, zested

Sea salt, to taste

Freshly ground black pepper

SERVES: 4-6
PREP TIME: 10 MINS | COOK TIME: 30 MINS | TOTAL TIME: 40 MINS

Heat a wide and shallow pan over medium-high heat. Add 2 tablespoons of oil, minced garlic, red pepper flakes and rice of choice. Sauté for 3 minutes.

Add the minced onion and cook for an additional 4-6 minutes.

Add the saffron threads, bay leaf, thyme, and water, and bring it to a boil. Bump it up to high heat. Once it's boiling, put a lid on the pan and reduce the heat to a simmer.

While that's simmering, sauté the mushrooms over high heat in the remaining 3 tablespoons of olive oil for 6-8 minutes until they are browned. Season with salt and pepper (mix it up with white pepper!). Remove from the pan and set aside.

Sauté the bell pepper in the leftover shroomy oil.

Dump the shrooms and bell peppers into the paella pan and stir to combine.

Sprinkle the lemon zest over the paella, and then cover the pan again for an additional 5 minutes.

Remove from heat, garnish with fresh thyme, and serve with some carny goodness of choice - crusty bread is always a winner.

MUJADDARA MY WAY

2 cups olive oil

1 cup lentils (*Any kind of lentil but red or yellow. They will turn to mush. No bueno. I like French lentils best because they hold up and they're so cute and tiny.*)

1 cup wild rice (*Traditionally it's short brown, but wild is better. And rice is better than rice substitutes for this recipe.*)

1 large yellow onion, sliced into thin rings

Sea salt to taste

Fresh squeezed lemon to serve

Water to cover the rice/lentils

SERVES: 4-6
PREP TIME: 5 MINS | COOK TIME: 25 MINS | TOTAL TIME: 30 MINS

This is so simple, yet so foodgasmic. It can be served as a main dish, as a side or even on top of a salad or avo toast. We never get tired of this one, and friends will come over asking if I have any made they can snack on. It's THAT good!

Pour the olive oil into a large pot. You read that right: 2 cups of olive oil and no substitutes. Separate and add the onion rings to the oil. Turn the heat up to medium high. You're going to blacken those onions. You should have about an inch of oil in the pot before the onion rings go in. You definitely want a lid because hot oil splatters. The onions take about 10 min to blacken. Stir occasionally to make sure they all go black.

Line a plate with a clean oil trapping towel of choice. Very carefully, scoop the onions out of the hot oil (very, very, very carefully, but worth every burn I've gotten over the years) and plop on the towel.

Reduce the oil heat to medium. Slowly and carefully pour in the lentils and rice. Fill with enough water to cover and put a lid on it.

Let cook for 10-15 minutes until the rice is done. Do not lift the lid before that. No peeking. The rice and lentils will soak up all the oil (hello flavor!) and water (plump AF).

Serve hot (or cold) with a drizzle of olive oil, a generous squeeze of lemon, a crack of fresh pepper, and a sprinkling of sea salt.

TIP:

Try leftovers cold over arugula with some of my "Parmesan" (pg 115). This is lunch on repeat for me.

COCONUT CEVICHE

1 ½ pounds coconut meat, sliced and/or chunked (*this mimics the fishy bits in texture*)

½ cup red pepper julienned thinly

¼ cup cilantro, chopped

2 tablespoons jalapeño, chopped, seeded

½ cup tomato, chopped

¼ cup red onion, chopped

½ cup cucumber, chopped

1 teaspoon garlic powder

1 tablespoon lime juice

½ tablespoon lemon juice

½ teaspoon black pepper

½ teaspoon sea salt

Avocado slices to garnish

SERVES: 4
PREP TIME: 10 MINS | TOTAL TIME: 10 MINS

This one is a quickie. Getting and preparing the ingredients is the hardest part. Simply dump everything in a bowl, toss it around to mix, serve, and enjoy.

Pour yourself a glass of wine.

Watch the sunset.

STUFFED PEPPERS

Extra virgin olive oil

1 medium yellow onion, minced

1 stalk celery, minced

2 pounds mushrooms (*half chopped, half sliced*)

¼ cup parsley, chopped, loosely packed

2 cloves garlic, minced

½ pound chopped frozen spinach

1 cup broccoli, chopped

1 teaspoon garlic powder

1 teaspoon onion powder

2 bay leaves

1 tablespoon basil, dried

1 tablespoon dill, dried

1 cup parmesan (*pg 115*)

½ teaspoon sea salt

6 grinds black pepper

1 ½ cups sauce tomat (*pg 119*) (*or your fave store bought marinara will do*)

8 bell peppers, tops cut off and insides ripped out

SERVES: 4-8
PREP TIME: 15 MINS | COOK TIME: 16 MINS | TOTAL TIME: 55-60 MINS

These babies are relatively easy to make. You can even buy pre-chopped veggies, or throw them all in a food processor to pulse. Don't get too small or you won't have veggie chunks to give texture.

————————

Preheat the oven to 350 F.

In a large skillet, over medium heat, swirl around the olive oil 6 to 8 times to generously coat the skillet.

Add in the onion, celery and mushrooms, and then sauté until onions are translucent. About 8 minutes.

Toss in everything BUT the bell peppers and cook, stirring occasionally, for 15-20 minutes.

Place the bell peppers on a lined baking sheet. Using a big spoon, ladle or even a measuring cup, scoop the filling mix and stuff each pepper to the brim with the mix.

Cook the stuffed peppers in the oven for 30 minutes.

NON-TRADITIONAL (PLANT-BASED) KEFTEDES

1 pint cremini mushrooms

½ cup walnuts

½ cup pistachios

½ cup sunflower seeds

1 yellow onion, minced

6 cloves garlic, crushed

½ cup almond flour

1 tablespoon olive oil

1 tablespoon chickpea flour

2 teaspoons dried oregano

2 teaspoons coriander

2 teaspoons cumin

½ teaspoon white pepper

1 teaspoon Mediterranean sea salt

4 tablespoons olive oil

3 tablespoons fresh lemon juice

5 sprigs fresh oregano

PARSLEY MINT TAHINI DRESSING

1 cup chopped parsley

½ cup mint leaves

1 tablespoon shallot, minced

½ tablespoon garlic, minced

Sea salt to taste

½ cup olive oil

½ cup lemon juice

3 tablespoons dry white wine vinegar

SERVES: 4-6
PREP TIME: 10 MINS | COOK TIME: 40 MINS | TOTAL TIME: 50 MINS

_____

Process all the keftedes ingredients together in a food processor until it reaches a ground meat-like consistency.

Using your hands or an ice cream scoop, form the mixture into 1 ½ to 2" size balls. Heehee, I said balls. #boymom

Heat the olive oil and lemon juice in a large skillet over medium heat. Add the "meatballs" to the skillet in a single layer with a tiny bit of space between. Nestle the oregano sprigs in between/over the keftedes (balls!!) and place a lid on the skillet.

Cook for 20 minutes and then flip the "meatballs" and cook for 10 more covered.

Uncover the skillet and cook for 10 more minutes.

While the balls are cooking, whip out the blender and whiz all the dressing ingredients together, which is also foodgasmic as a salad dressing! You're welcome.

VACON MUSHROOM SCALLOPS

24 portobello mushroom stems

1 tablespoon sea salt

3 tablespoons fresh squeezed lemon juice

3 sprigs fresh thyme

3 tablespoons oil (*same kind used in the vacon*)

1 clove garlic, minced (*about 1 teaspoon*)

1 small shallot, minced (*about 2 tablespoons*)

Quick grind of fresh black pepper

vacon (*pg. 24*)

GARNISH

Fresh lemon zest

Fresh thyme leaves

SERVES: 2-4
PREP TIME: 10 MINS | COOK TIME: 10 MINS | TOTAL TIME: 20 MINS

The exact recipe I did on Food Network's Guy's Grocery Games with Guy Fieri. These babies blew everyone away. And they're super quick. I shopped, cooked, plated, and served these in under 30 minutes. They LOOK fancy and intimidating, but it's way more difficult to mess these up than you'd think. I walked a never-cooks-in-her-life friend through making these on the phone from shopping to eating, including walking home from the grocery store. She was done in 45 minutes. I like to stuff my face, so I generally do a dozen large mushroom "scallops" per person.

Fun fact: These babies are sodamngood that my "friend turned foe" on GGG invited me out to his hometown in Arkansas to have me show them off. Hi Brent!

———————————

Mix all the marinade ingredients together and let sit for UP TO 10 minutes

Wash the mushroom stems and shake dry. If uneven - or if you're a tad OCD like me and need #instaworthy perfect little rounds - trim the top and bottom of each stem and peel or cut off any ridges that might be on the larger size.

Generously sprinkle the tops and bottoms of the slightly damp stems with sea salt. Let that sit and make the "bacon" bits (pg. 24).

In a clean frying pan (sorry, can't re-use the same pan here), sauté the garlic, shallot, sea salt, pepper, and thyme over medium heat.

Use tongs to carefully place each mushroom stem in the pan, flat side down. Let cook for 3 minutes, flip then cook for 2 minutes on the other side. Carefully add in the lemon juice and immediately cover with a lid to steam everything for 1 to 2 minutes.

Place the scallops on plate(s) and garnish with fresh lemon zest, bacon impersonating zucchini, and thyme.

TIP:

On the show, I couldn't get the wine. They're delicious without it, but sometimes you want that extra oomph, in which case a splash of dry white wine into the pan instead of the lemon juice will do. I just slosh some out of the bottle. Walking my sister through the recipe a few times, we decided 1 ounce is the appropriate amount.

BURGER TO DIE FOR

4 fluffy gluten-free brioche or potato buns

4 @beyondmeat burger patty (*4 ounces each*)

4 slices choice American flavor cheese (*13g per burger is the proper proportion*)

8 thin slices beefsteak tomato (*2 slices per burger, 1cm thick slice, approximately 10g each*)

8 leaves Bibb lettuce (*Boston in a pinch - 9g per burger is ideal*)

4 teaspoons Miyokos Creamery butter

4 tablespoons spicy brown mustard

1 teaspoon fave cooking oil (*I used avocado*)

SERVES: 2-4
PREP TIME: 2 MINS | COOK TIME: 3 MINS | TOTAL TIME: 5 MINS

That might be a slight over exaggeration, but it IS a delicious fucking burger. Did you know there is actually a science to building the perfect burger? It's NOT just throw a patty on a bun with some condiments and call it a day. It's the reason some burgers you remember forever, and others you're like, why TF am I eating this thing? I encourage creativity in the kitchen, always, but the first time you make this, please follow the directions and ingredients exactly for the scientifically perfect burger. I've also included fail-proof alternates to mix it up to really impress, from "cowboy" style burger to a shroom burger, all the hits can be found right here.

This will be a controversial statement: The BEST burgers are NOT made on a grill, but on a cast iron on the stove top - never press a burger, you want ALL those flavors IN the patty, and no where to drip off to. You can totes grill out if you want, but we are going for optimal flavor not manliness and fire fun here. So I recommend cast iron, and I stand by that statement. I've not tried a cast iron skillet ON the grill. Yet. If you do, let me know how it goes, and grill responsibly (don't touch the cast iron!). When cooking with cast irons, they get hot AF, so you'll need to ventilate with the range fan on high and likely open the doors and/or windows. As The Mask (Jim Carrey fans anyone?) would say: Saaaahmmmooooooookey.

_____

Heat a pan (cast iron highly recommended or flat top grill option on the stovetop if you have it) over medium-high heat. Add the oil and drop the patties on it. Cook for 2-3 minutes.

While the patty is cooking, toast your buns.

Plop the brown mustard on top of the burger patty, then flip it (that's the chef secret to making burgers taste AH-MAZING!) and cook it for 2 more minutes. Unless you're allergic to mustard, do NOT skip the mustard. If you're cooking burgers on a grill, you can skip the mustard, because you're also skipping a lot of flavor by letting it drip down into the grill. At least you're adding some "smoke" flavor, right?

Spread the European style butter on the cut side of each side of your bun.

Place the slice of American cheese on top of the patty and cover the pan with a lid. Turn off the heat and let the cheese melt for 1-2 minutes.

While the cheese is melting, whisk together the special sauce ingredients.

Layer like a pro: Bun, burger patty with melted cheese on top, lettuce, tomato, then add the toasted buttered top half of the bun.

The most scientifically perfect assembly goes like this, building from the bottom up:

Plain burger: bottom bun, patty, (red onion slices, or caramelized onion if adding), lettuce, tomato, (pickles if adding), (special sauce if adding), top bun

Cheese burger: bottom bun, patty, (red onion slices, or caramelized onion if adding), cheese, lettuce, tomato, (pickles if adding), (special sauce if adding), top bun

MIX IT UP AND MAKE IT FANCY:

Cowboy burger: bottom bun, patty, caramelized onion, chili or black beans, cheese, seared hatch or poblano pepper, special sauce, top bun

Guac burger: bottom bun, 1 tablespoon chipotle mayo, patty, red onion slices, lettuce, tomato, guacamole, tortilla chips, salsa, top bun

Shroom burger: bottom bun, marinated portobello mushroom "patty", red onion if using, cheese (can use cheddar flavor OR sub with provolone flavor), lettuce, tomato, special sauce, top bun

SPECIAL SAUCE RECIPE:

cup mayo

4 tablespoons ketchup

4 tablespoons sweet relish

4 tablespoons apple cider vinegar

2 teaspoons lemon juice

4 teaspoon pepper (white to hide, black for tradition)

4 teaspoon sea salt

For the secret sauce: mix ingredients well to combine and then keep refrigerated

CARAMELIZED ONION:

1 large white onion, diced

2 tablespoons oil to cook (avocado)

½ teaspoon sea salt

½ teaspoon black pepper

4 ounces water

To make the perfect caramelized, but fluffy onions: heat the oil in a skillet over medium high heat. Add in the onion, sea salt and pepper. If the onion mix gets dry, add in water 1 tablespoon at a time as needed, until the onions are soft/brown/caramelized.

SUPA-DUPA QUICK & EASY CHIPOTLE MAYO:

1 cup mayo

¼ teaspoon chipotle powder

⅛ teaspoon paprika

¼ teaspoon apple cider vinegar

To make: mix ingredients together until supa-dupa combined.

PORTOBELLO MUSHROOM PATTY:

4 portobello mushroom caps, cleaned and ridges removed (scrape the bottom side out)

½ cup avocado oil (can use olive)

3 tablespoons chopped white or yellow onions

3 tablespoons minced garlic

½ cup coconut aminos

To make: place the mushrooms in a bag, fill with other ingredients, shake it up, and seal airtight. Let marinate at LEAST 1 hour, but ideally "overnight" (8-14 hours).

PULLED BBQ SANDWICH

16 ounces jackfruit (*vacuum sealed or canned in water*) OR 1 pound of oyster mushrooms

1 ½ cups BBQ sauce (*see my recipe pg. 123, or use your fave store bought. If going raw/vegan see recipe below for what we used at my restaurant*)

4 slices bread of choice

Pickle slices (*optional*)

COLESLAW

2 cups shredded cabbage (*any color, but I like mixing purple and green*)

1 cup mayo (*my recipe, pg. 121, or store bought for even quicker*)

1 tablespoon apple cider vinegar

1 teaspoon dijon mustard

SERVES: 2
PREP TIME: 5 MINS | COOK TIME: 15 MINS | TOTAL TIME: 20 MINS

This was a huge hit in my restaurant and this version is ridiculously fast and easy to make. If you REALLY want, you can break open some jackfruits. I've included tips on that, but you can find them vacuum sealed in the fridge section or packed in water in the pantry section of just about any grocery store now. If you can't find jackfruit, use oyster mushrooms. Directions for both are included here, both are equally delicious. The jackfruit will keep for a few days in an airtight container in the fridge, but the oyster mushroom variation must be eaten within 30 minutes or it WILL get mush. Gag.

Jackfruit: Thoroughly rinse the jackfruit. Mix with the BBQ sauce and shred using 2 forks.

Oyster mushrooms: Thoroughly wash, drain, and pat dry with a clean dish towel or paper towels. Mix with the BBQ sauce and shred using 2 forks.

Mix together the coleslaw ingredients until well combined.

Place 1 cup of coleslaw mix on 2 slices of bread.

Top with 1 cup of BBQ jackfruit mix.

Top with other slice of bread.

Slice corner to corner so the sandwich looks larger and prettier.

SO YOU WANNA BE A BALLER AND TAKE A WHACK AT AN ACTUAL, STRAIGHT FROM THE WILD, JACKFRUIT:

BUYING TIPS: You'll want YOUNG jackfruit. This means the entire thing should be green. You can find them in health food stores, but your best bet for quality and price is an asian grocer.

When it is ripe, it will have black spots, be very fragrant (ripe has an incredibly strong and distinct smell), and have a bright yellow interior flesh. You do NOT want that for this recipe, or it will taste like jackfruit covered in BBQ sauce. NOT what you want here. Ripe jackfruit is very sweet, like mango sweet (it IS a tropical fruit), unripe is bland AF and texture wise mimics shredded meat, so it's great for this recipe. You'll also want to pack some guns. I'm talking biceps not firearms. These suckers are big and heavy like watermelon.

CUTTING TIPS: Stand the jackfruit up on one end so it's taller than wide, and cut down the center with a very large knife and sturdy hands and strong grasp. Once split in two, use a knife to cut out the flesh. You CAN eat the little pod seed things (the groups of flesh are the "pods" while the seeds are massive and look like their own pod to me). For this recipe you'll want to extract them for the most shredded meat-like consistency and texture. If your goal is not to replicate meat, leave them - we did at my restaurant. They're packed with nutrients!

STORAGE: These suckers are MASSIVE, if you're not feeding a crowd, you will have leftovers. The cut fruit will keep in the fridge in an airtight container for up to 5 days. Mixed with sauce or not, it's still 5 days tops (the sauce below only lasts 3 days, so if you're using that recipe, and you mixed it all together, consume at your own risk after 3 days.)

SPICY TUNO TOWER

1 cup water

2 tablespoons sesame oil

2 tablespoons sriracha

2 tablespoons paprika

1 tablespoon chili powder

1 teaspoon ginger powder

¼ teaspoon sea salt

6-8 medium firm tomatoes (*eg. larger Roma, hothouse*)

½ teaspoon coconut aminos (*optional*)

For peeling the tomatoes: Boiling water (*enough to cover tomatoes, I use instant hot water, it's about 4 cups*)

2 avocados

1 teaspoon lemon juice

Pinch sea salt

2 cups mango chunks (*thawed frozen works great*)

2 cups pineapple chunks (*thawed frozen works*)

GARNISH

Micro greens and/or edible flowers (*optional*)

MAKES: 4
PREP TIME: 5 MINS | COOK TIME: 15 MINS | TOTAL TIME: 20 MINS

This step is actually easy, even though it will read intimidatingly. Score an "X" on the bottom of each tomato. This makes it easier to peel. Place the tomatoes in a large bowl, and fill with enough boiling water to cover. Let sit for 5 minutes, until the tomato corners of the "X" start to lift. Remove the tomatoes and peel the skins off. Dice the tomatoes, removing the core.

Whisk together the water and spices. Add in the tomatoes and let marinate for a few minutes while making the rest or can be made a day in advance. The marinated tomatoes only keep in an airtight container in the fridge for 3 days tops.

In a small bowl, smash together the avocado, lemon juice, and sea salt. Set aside.

To layer, place a 4-6 inch diameter ring on the plate. Press ¼ cup each of the mango and pineapple into the bottom. Add ½ cup of the tuno and ¼ of the avocado mixture. Carefully expand the ring to remove, garnish and repeat for the other 3 towers.

FUN ALTERNATIVE:

If the pineapple and mango is too sweet and/or mushy for you, sub it out with chopped cucumber and/or jicama. Mix with ½ - 1 tablespoon of finely chopped parsley and ½ - 1 tablespoon of finely chopped cilantro and a squeeze of lime.

WATERMELON PIZZA

1 seedless watermelon, turned on it's side and sliced into 1 ½ to 2" thick rounds

SAUCE

cashew/coconut cream sauce (pg. 125)

TOPPINGS (*small handful of each*)

Raspberries

Blackberries

Strawberries

Sliced figs

Microgreens

Edible flowers

Fresh herbs (*I'm obsessed with lemon verbena on these!*)

Cinnamon (*sprinkle/dust on top - no handfuls of this one. Not going for the cinnamon challenge*)

Peach slices (*even grilled - or grill the whole thing!*)

Plum slices

Arugula for some bite

Kiwi

Chocolate sauce (*pg. 124*)

Avocado

Tomatoes

Nuts & seeds

SERVES: 2-6 DEPENDING ON APPETITE
PREP TIME: 10-20 MINS | TOTAL TIME: 10-20 MINS

Please, please, please get creative here! In no way are you limited by the ingredients below, only your imagination! F*ck it, you could even blow someone's mind by going savory with olives, fresh basil, fresh oregano and some feta! Dump a salad on top and spread it around to make it pretty!

Drizzle (or slather) the watermelon rounds in cream of your choice.

Top with toppings of choice.

Slice into pizza slices

Serve and enjoy!

JUST THE TIP

Stuff blueberries into raspberries for a pretty look.

Keep on or de-leaf the strawberries, then using a paring knife, go one-third of the way up the strawberry. Hold the knife so the side of the tip of the blade is against the strawberry and carefully press in and down to make a little horizontal strip you can carefully pull/roll out to make a flower petal design with. Repeat that little cut on the other three "sides." Then go up closer to the pointed tip of the strawberry and make a cut between the lower petal cuts, repeating until the whole strawberry is done.

Slice fruit in different ways for more visual appeal (rounds, wedges, slivers, or cubes) or go all out with mini cookie cutter shapes and make it next level #instaworthy. You will most definitely need to tag me on that so I can see your awesomeness!

DESSERTS

SEX CHOCOLATES

1 cup finely chopped/grated cocoa butter

½ cup cacao powder

½ cup monkfruit granules

1 teaspoon vanilla extract
Pinch of sea salt

1 tablespoon maca powder

2 teaspoons horny goat weed powder

1 teaspoon ashwagandha powder

1 teaspoon shatavari powder

1 dropper CBD oil (*no flavor*)

MAKES: 1 POUND
COOK TIME: 10 MINS | SET TIME: 20 MIN+ | TOTAL TIME: 30 MINS

*Adaptogenic aphrodisiac chocolates. Fuck yes. These potent little babies will balance your body and get you feelin' frisky. I created these for Valentine's Day at my restaurant one year, and had people calling, texting and DMing me to place orders in huge batches. They work. You've been warned. Enjoy! *sly smile**

In a large saucepan, bring 2 inches of water to boil over medium high heat. Set a medium glass, ceramic or stainless mixing bowl on top, making sure it does not touch the water. If you have one, you can use a double boiler instead.

Add chopped cocoa butter to your bowl and let melt, about 2 minutes.

Once melted, add monk fruit granules one 1 tablespoon at a time and whisk or stir to mix until completely incorporated before adding the next tablespoon. This is important, or your chocolate will be grainy!

Remove bowl from heat.

Add cacao powder, vanilla and sea salt, and whisk to combine until completely smooth.

Add Maca and whisk smooth.

Add horny goat weed and whisk smooth.

Add ashwagandha and whisk smooth.

Add shatavari and whisk smooth.

Finally, add in CBD oil and whisk smooth.

Pour into chocolate/candy molds, or if you're feeling extra frisky, into cupcake/muffin tins.

Leave as is, or garnish with sea salt, lavender, rose petals, nuts, seeds, or gold dust. Your call!

TIP:

TTC? (That's "Trying To Conceive") Boost those swimmers by turning these into chocolate covered espresso beans. Plop little espresso beans into the mold with the chocolate (you can find chocolate covered espresso bean molds online), pour in the chocolate, plop in the bean and chill. Consume 20 minutes before the estimated swimmer release time for maximum speed.

LEMON SORBET

1 cup granulated sweetener (*I use monkfruit*)

1 cup filtered water

2 teaspoons fresh lemon zest

1 cup freshly squeezed lemon juice (*meyer lemons make the absolute best!*)

2 teaspoons limoncello (*optional*)

GARNISH

Fresh mint leaves

Lemon zest

SERVES: 4
PREP TIME: 30 MINS | CHILL TIME: 1 HR | TOTAL TIME: 1 HR 30 MINS

Not so secret: I love making desserts, and smelling them. Top secret: I don't actually have much of a sweet tooth. My kids definitely do, but I prefer the savory and spicy. I do, however, love lemon sorbet. I've included options to make with or without an ice cream maker.

_____

In a saucepan over medium-high heat, heat the sweetener, water and zest until the sweetener has completely dissolved.

Remove from the heat and strain, let it cool for a bit. Note: You can leave the zest in for pretty speckles, or strain out the lemon zest for that smooth creamy look.

Mix in the lemon juice (and limoncello if using), and place in the fridge to chill completely.

Once cool, follow the instructions for your ice cream maker.

If you don't have an ice cream maker, pour the mixture into a shallow pan and freeze until semi-solid. Use a fork to scrape and fluff it up then freeze again until firm and frozen. Put it through a food processor to blend smooth before serving.

Scoop it out and garnish with fresh mint.

RASPBERRY MANGO SORBET

1 pound frozen raspberries

1 pound frozen mango

2 tablespoons fresh lime juice (you *can* sub orange or lemon, but keep it fresh squeezed)

SERVES: 2-4
TOTAL TIME: 5 MINS

It's madness how easy this is to make. It's pure fruit, no sweeteners and absolutely perfect.

_____

Purée all ingredients in a food processor until smooth. Serve immediately.

If you're posting your creation online, throw in a few fresh raspberries, and maybe some mint because it's green, a complementary color, and adds a visual "freshness" when seen.

SALTED CARAMELS

CARAMELS

2 cups cashews

3 cups pitted dates, chopped

CHOCOLATE SAUCE

⅔ cup coconut oil, melted

1 cup cacao powder

1/2 cup maple syrup

1/4 teaspoon vanilla

Pinch of sea salt

GARNISH

Sea salt (*I like fleur de sel*)

Dried edible lavender (*optional*)

Dried edible roses (*optional*)

SERVES: 12
PREP TIME: 10 MINS | COOK TIME: 20 MINS | TOTAL TIME: 30 MINS

Few will believe these have none of the traditional caramel ingredients, because it has ALL of the caramel flavor. And, they take way less effort to make. #winning These are the same salted caramels I served in my restaurant and made on Guy's Grocery Games on Food Network. As a kid, I loved caramels. My great grandmother would give them to me, and so I associate them with fond memories. I created these so my dairy sensitive child could enjoy some similar memories.

———————

For the chocolate sauce: Blend all the chocolate sauce ingredients together in a high powered blender, until smooth.

For the caramels: Put cashews in a food processor and grind into a flour, slowly add in the dates, while the food processor is running, one or two at a time. Once all of the dates have been added, keep it running for 3-5 minutes until you have a ball of caramel rolling around in the food processor.

Spread the sticky deliciousness about 1 inch thick on a parchment paper lined cookie sheet. Place in the fridge to harden, about 20 minutes.

Remove and cut into small 1 inch-ish sized squares.

Sprinkle with sea salt. To serve you can put on a bed of chocolate sauce, or zig zag it on the top.

If using sprinkle with dried lavender and/or roses.

LEMON CHEESECAKE

CRUST

2 cups almonds

1 pinch sea salt

8 pitted dates, chopped (*medjool best*)

GARNISH

Lemon slices and/or zest (*optional*)

FILLING

3 cups raw cashews, rinsed under hot water

1 cup fresh squeezed lemon juice

⅔ cup coconut oil, melted

1 cup maple syrup

2 tablespoons sunflower lecithin

SERVES: 4
TOTAL TIME: 3 HRS

Creamy, zingy and even magical... plus you don't have to cook anything!

———————

For the crust: In a food processor, process the sea salt and almonds until it's a slightly chunky flour-like consistency.

While running, slowly add the dates until the mixture is crumbly.

Press the crust into a greased springform pan (or line a Pyrex dish with anything that will allow you to pop the cheesecake out). Make sure to press the crust mix evenly and flat across the bottom so the cheesecake comes out nice.

For the filling: Blend all ingredients together until smooth. Or, if you need an arm workout, use an old school mixing bowl and whisk combo. Make sure to post on IG and tag me so I can see your badass cooking skills and rock hard bicep.

Pour the filling mix over the crust in the prepped pan. Place in the fridge to set for a few hours, depending on the height of your pan, shallow set quicker and taller take longer). If you're like my kids check on it regularly and swipe the top with your (clean) fingers to taste test. When people ask why the cake looks funny, say it's art and grin knowing you got more cheesecake than anyone else.

TIP:

Place pancakes on each plate, top with a beautiful blob of butter, a generous drizzle of maple syrup and a sprinkling of lemon zest.

TARTE TARTIN

SHORTCRUST PASTRY

1 ½ cups gluten-free flour (*I mix half cassava half almond*)

1 cup granulated sweetener (*I use monkfruit*)

5 tablespoons butter of choice (*I love Miyokos Creamery*)

1 pinch sea salt

1 [v]egg (*I generally use Bob's Redmill for ease*)

APPLE TARTE FILLING

3 ½ pounds apples, cored & sliced in wedge (*nice firm ones like Braeburn, Pink lady & Honeycrisp*)

5 ½ tablespoons butter of choice, chopped

½ cup granulated sweetener

SERVES: 6-8
PREP TIME: 10 MINS | COOK TIME: 55-75 MINS | TOTAL TIME: 65-85 MINS

It's hard to go wrong with shortcrust pastry and tender juicy apples. This crowd-pleaser is easy to make, and fun to do as a group project with your partner, friends or kids. The traditional way is to make it upside-down, with apples on the bottom so they're extra caramelized and crust on top. Then you flip it out to serve. It tastes amazing both ways, but I prefer a more tart tarte with the crust on bottom. Plus, it's 20 minutes quicker to make that way. I'll explain both methods to making it so you can mix it up.

For the pastry: Preheat the oven to 350 F.

In a large mixing bowl, combine the flour, sugar, butter and sea salt, mixing and mashing it all together with your hands (enlist a child for this!), until it's fine and crumbly.

Add the [v]egg and knead just enough to incorporate and form a ball. If it's too dry to form a ball, add just a touch of water (1 teaspoon at a time) until you can ball it. Let it rest in the fridge and move on to the apples.

For the filling: Over medium heat, melt the butter and granulated sweetener on the stove top, bringing to a slight simmer. Stir often until it's a nice golden color, about 10-15 minutes. Going rebellious? Skip ahead to the "For You Rebels".

If you're going traditional, pour that caramel into a 9-10 inch diameter tart pan, then pack a layer of apple slices in tightly on top of it. Add a second layer of apples, filling in all the gaps, then bake for 20 minutes.

Back to the pastry dough: Remove from the fridge, and roll the dough out on a floured surface, so it's 10-11 inches in diameter.

Lay the pastry over the apples in the tart, using a spatula to press the outer edge down against the caramelizing apples. Give it a few pricks with a fork and stick it back in the oven for 25 minutes.

If serving soon, turn the heat off, and let sit in the oven for another 20-30 minutes. Then remove from the oven and let cool to lukewarm on the counter before turning it out.

If you're serving later, you can stick it in the fridge, then heat it before serving at 300 F for 15-20 minutes. Remove from the oven and let cool to the touch before flipping out on a plate.

To flip: Run a knife around the edges to separate the crust if needed. Turn the serving plate upside down over the tart dish, holding it together firmly with your hands (make sure it has cooled to lukewarm, so it's easier to slip out but won't burn you), quickly and carefully lift the tart pan and plate and flip it over so the plate is now on the bottom and tart pan on top. Carefully remove the tart pan to reveal your beautiful tarte tatin.

FOR YOU REBELS OR ONES IN A HURRY: Remove the pastry dough from the fridge, and press it into the bottom of a lightly greased 9-10 inch tart pan or round baking dish.

Layer the apples in a tightly packed layer, not leaving any gaps. Spoon a little of the caramelized butter mixture over. Tightly pack a second layer, no gaps - even if you have to use smaller apple pieces. Spoon the rest of the caramelized butter mixture over the top. Bake for 35-40 minutes.

Let cool and serve.

PAIN AU CHOCOLAT

Puff Pastry Dough *(pg. 32)*

CHOCOLAT[E]

10 ounces bittersweet chocolate, solid, chopped

"EGG" WASH*

2 tablespoons almond milk

1 tablespoon maple syrup

Note: very few store bought egg substitutes work as an egg wash. The few that come looking like uncooked scrambled eggs do, but the above will work and get that golden crust too.

SERVES: 6-12 DEPENDING ON SMALL OR LARGE
PREP TIME: A LONG ASS TIME - ABOUT 1 HR 30 MINS TO 2 HRS DEPENDING ON SPEED AND CHILL TIME | PROOF TIME: 2 TO 3 HRS | COOK TIME: 8-10 MINS | TOTAL TIME: #WORTHIT 2HRS 38 MINS TO 5 HRS 10 MINS

One of the greatest inventions of all time: flaky croissant filled with gooey chocolate. Pain au chocolat translates from French to English as "bread with chocolate" and is pronounced "pahn oh show-koh-lah." It's wrapped in croissants (that amazing flaky puff pastry dough), while we're at it, that's pronounced "Kwah-sohn" with a tiny touch of a guttural sound on the K. Like a kitty cat purring - or like you're trying to secretly clear the top of your throat by the epiglottis (AKA the hangy ball thingy) while speaking.

———————————

Now to turn the Puff Pastry into PAIN AU CHOCOLAT: Remove the now hardened puff pastry from the fridge/freezer.

Using a sharp knife, cut the dough into 3 ½-ish by 4 ½-ish inch rectangles. Lightly dust your work surface with cassava flour, and lay each rectangle out on the surface, with the long side facing you.

Now we add the chocolate! Line the upper third of each rectangle with about ½ TB of the chopped chocolate. Fold that third of the dough over the chocolate.

Place another ½-ish tablespoon of the chocolate along the seam of the folded part of the dough. Then fold the bottom third of the pastry dough up over the chocolate, it can overlap on the other part of the dough too, we're not making binoculars here. If you're not wanting to make & eat them all right away, maybe you're making these in advance for a party, or like me, have little self control around pain au chocolat *swoon* - this is the stage where they can be wrapped and sealed air tight then frozen for up to a week.

If you freeze these babies, you'll want to thaw them out on a parchment paper-covered baking sheet overnight in the refrigerator before baking.

Flip each pain au chocolat (I love saying it almost as I love eating it!) over, so the seams face down. This keeps them from opening up as they fluff up while baking. Transfer these beauties to a parchment paper lined baking sheet, about 2 inches apart - they will get bigger as they bake. Loosely cover the baking sheet with a clean kitchen towel so the pain au chocolat can "proof" at room temperature for 2-3 hours until they have doubled in size and appear light and full of air

Preheat the oven to 400 degrees.

Make the "egg wash" by whisking together the almond milk and maple syrup in a small bowl until well combined. Using a pastry brush (in a pinch you can grab a clean napkin in the center, and pull it so the corners all meet at the bottom, then dip the tip of that center in the wash mix), very, very gently (especially if using a napkin) coat the entire tops of each pain au chocolat with the wash.

Bake until they get that nice golden brown crust, about 8-10 minutes.

Baking science says if you have any leftovers they can be stored for up to 2 weeks in the freezer if wrapped and sealed air tight. I've never had success with this, the closest I got was a few days before my boys devoured the "cool chocolate croissant popsicles."

If you do freeze the final product, thaw them at room temperature and warm in the oven before serving.

CREME BRULEE

2 cans full fat unsweetened coconut milk

¼ cup tapioca flour (you can use arrowroot if you have, or even corn starch)

¼ cup liquid sweetener (maple syrup is my go to)

1 teaspoon agar powder (online or health food stores)

2 ½ teaspoons vanilla

¼ teaspoon sea salt

2 tablespoons granular sweetener (I use monkfruit)

SERVES: 4
PREP TIME: 5 MINS | COOK TIME: 15 MINS | SET TIME: 2 HRS | TORCH/BROILER TIME: 2-4 MINS | TOTAL TIME: 2 HRS 22 MINS TO 2 HRS 24 MINS

These are so delicious and worth the "weird" ingredients and blow torch. If you don't have a blow torch, you can use the broiler setting on your oven, but I most def recommend getting one because they're relatively cheap and a lot of fun! Probably too much fun. The "weird" ingredients (tapioca to thicken and agar to gelatinize) are what set these up so they are thick and creamy and have the proper consistency.

For the Creme Brulee: Blend all of the ingredients together until smooth.

Pour the blender mix into a medium-sized saucepan over medium-low heat.

Cook, whisking frequently, until it's thickened, about 10 to 15 minutes. It will resemble pudding when ready.

NOTE: Do NOT let it come to a boil, that will "ruin" it. So if you see a bubble, or "feel" like a bubble is coming, turn down the heat.

Line a baking dish with 4 to 6 ramekins (depending on the size), and evenly distribute the creme brulee mix between the ramekins. Let sit on the counter to cool for an hour.

After cooled, transfer to the fridge to firm up more, for at least one more hour.

When ready to serve, dust with the granular sweetener and hit with the blow torch, or place on the top rack in the oven under the broiler for 4 minutes. Serve immediately.

PEANUT BUTTER FUDGE

1 ½ cup lakanto monkfruit sweetener, classic (*white*)

½ cup water

1 cup buttah (*Miyokos or bust IMHO & def salted*)

4 cups unsweetened creamy peanut butter (*just peanuts, nothing added*)

4 cups lakanto sugar free powdered monkfruit sweetener

SERVES: 1 HAPPY GREAT GRANDFATHER | MAKES: 5 LBS - 1 HALF SHEET PAN (YOUR TRADITIONAL HOME SIZED RIMMED BAKING SHEET)
COOK TIME: 10 MINS | CHILL TIME: 30-ISH MIN | TOTAL TIME: 40 MINS

When I was a kid, I'd make this during summer visits with my great grandmother. She used to make it for her son, my grandfather, who is the grandest of all the granddaddies. Now, I make it every year for his birthday. What else do you give the man who has everything? The taste of childhood - food has that power. BUT, I want to keep him healthy, and he lives a very healthy lifestyle--he's a super cyclist, in his 80s. The original recipe had a lot of corn syrup. Like a LOT of corn syrup. Light color - never the dark, no substitutions. EVER. Sorry, not sorry grandma, I've subbed BIG TIME here, but I swear the quality is top notch and the flavor is the same! This recipe is super sweet, just like granddaddy, and just like he likes it.

In a large saucepan, over high heat, bring the monkfruit sweetener and water to a boil, and then reduce to a simmer (low heat), stirring occasionally until mostly dissolved. This mimics the corn syrup.

Add in the buttah, stirring until it's melted.

Add in the peanut butter, scraping every last bit out of the jar, stir so it's combined with the buttery syrupy goodness.

Through a mesh colander, sieve, strainer, anything, add in the powdered monkfruit sweetener. You really want to have it go in fluffy, or you'll wind up with powdered sugar balls in the fudge. Stir until it's all combined and remove from heat immediately. We're going with my great grandmother's method, no candy thermometers or dropping for balls needed.

Line your rimmed baking tray with parchment paper, spread the fudge on top in an even layer. Place in the fridge to harden.

Cut into 1 inch square pieces. It keeps forever in the fridge, having done my food safety certifications for the restaurants, let's eat it within a month, and freeze for up to 3 months. It will keep in a cool spot on the counter for about a month if you can keep it away from my great grandfather.

[NO] SUGAR COOKIES

1 cup coconut oil

1 cup monkfruit

1 teaspoon vanilla

½ teaspoon almond extract

1 [v]egg of choice

2 teaspoons baking powder

½ teaspoon sea salt

2 cups almond flour

1 cup cassava flour

COOKIE ICING

8 ounces cream cheese

1 teaspoon vanilla

½ cup monkfruit

natural food coloring
(optional - kids like when i cut
stars and use yellow coloring
with gold dust)

DECOR

Anything you like. You can
add food coloring to the
icing and decorate for the
holidays, or just sprinkle with
some edible flowers like roses
and lavender.

MAKES: 24 COOKIES
PREP TIME: 10 MINS | BAKE TIME: 10 MINS | TOTAL TIME: 20 MINS

Wait, what? Yes, sugarless sugar cookies!! My kids and their friends LOVE these, and their traditional sugar cooking eating friends can't tell the difference!

So, so, so many people have tried to buy this recipe from me, intending to take it to market. And I suppose they still can, after reading this book, but you won't have to rely on their supply to enjoy these. I love reverse engineering items off shelves in grocery stores, but that's me. You probably don't. Here it is, my never before shared recipe for the best fucking sugar cookies ever. The no gluten and no sugar thing is just a bonus. Even better: there is zero chill time. Yippee!

Preheat the oven to 350 F.

For the dough: In a mixing bowl, cream the coconut oil, monk fruit, vanilla and almond extract together. Once creamed, add in the [v]egg and mix together to incorporate.

In a separate bowl, mix together the baking powder, sea salt, almond flour and cassava flour, then put through a mesh strainer of sorts, this will give you fluffier cookies, while not required, it gives a better texture

Add the flour mix to the cream mix and mix well.

Ball or roll out the dough. Yep, that's right, NO chilling required. Insert happy dance here.

Cut with cookie cutters or just press little 3 inch rounds down on a greased cookie sheet.

Bake for 8 minutes, remove from the oven, let cool for 2 minutes then transfer to a cooling rack.

For the icing: Mix all ingredients together in a mixer, or with a lot of elbow grease and a spoon or spatula.

CHOCOLATE CARAMEL CONCRETE

4 frozen bananas

2 ripe non frozen bananas

6 dates

1 teaspoon vanilla powder

1 teaspoon reishi powder

1 teaspoon maca powder

Aloe water (*just enough to blend smooth-ish*)

CHOCOLATE CHUNKS

1 whole CBD chocolate bar (50mg), broken up

CHOCOLATE SAUCE

½ cup cacao

¼ cup maple

¼ cup coconut oil, melted

1 teaspoon vanilla powder (*optional*)

1 dropper CBD oil (*optional*)

SERVES: 1-2
TOTAL TIME: 5 MINS

Invigorating + Refreshing Adaptogenic Chocolate NiceCream Concrete Shake. I like to make my food multitask and "do things" - so voila! A functional foods adaptogenic stress reducing energizing relaxing and grounding ice cream "smoothie" that is thick and delicious like an ultra magnificent concrete frozen custard.

_____

For the chocolate sauce: In a high powered blender, blend all ingredients smooth. Pour/drip/drizzle down the inside sides of the glass to create designs. Set in the fridge to keep chill and from pooling in the bottom of the glass.

For the concrete: In a clean blender (or not if you're not snapping photos for the Gram), blend all ingredients together until smooth. Add in a broken up chocolate bar, and pulse to combine and chop up a bit more.

Pour the caramel concrete mix into the chilled prepared glasses. Serve with a thick straw.

Holy shit, I am #gratefulAF. I am so very deeply thankful to so many amazing and wonderful people in my life.

A super-sized heart wide open hug to all the rockstars at Monkedia, especially the visionary Noah Curran, brilliant Kevin Kaiser and wonder woman Morganne Stewart. Thank you so much for coming along on this adventure and making magic with me.

Thank you to the ever talented & delightful Madison Bradley King for glamming me up.

To the rock stars behind the camera, the talented Jarrod Fresquez, thank you for capturing Foodgasm in all its glory on camera, and another thanks to the multitasking super human Morganne Stewart for making everything (and me!) look so freaking good.

My Boom Juice, Be Raw & IG fam: Thank you, thank you, thank you for all your love & support over the past 8 years.

To the one and only Guy Fieri & the entire team at GGG - a massive thank you for taking a chance and having this vegan chef cook all vegan, in a cooking competition, on TV, against meat, for meat eating judges, TWICE. I love a challenge, and had an absolute blast.

A giant thank you to David Alcaro, for putting your money where your mouth is and insisting people will pay me for my food. Your faith in me got me started on this journey - what a ride!

To all my friends that came over and tasted all my food, helping me curate the best recipes to put in my first cookbook. In particular Genevieve Gurchak & Lori Schlussel for encouraging me to FINALLY just do it, insisting my food was already perfect & for believing me in and knowing that I am the best there is at what I do. You ladies are rock stars.

Toni Najjar, no words, you are amazing & an inspiration. I love you.

To my OG soul sister: Kristi Redford, thank you for always being there for the last 3 decades. I love you.

Christopher, Sarah & Hannah: Thank you soul buddies, my three stars and the best siblings I could have ever hoped for. I love you.

Nana, Granddaddy, Grandma, Kate (& Joe), & Mom: Thank you for loving me and letting me be me - I know I can be a pain in the @$$, I get my strong will-power from you guys. *wink*

Thank you for being patient and also for trying all my "weird" non meat/dairy/gluten foods.

Thank you to my everythings, the humans this book and my life are dedicated to: Winston, Hudson & Sebastien. Thank you for teaching me the meaning of unconditional love. Thank you for being patient with me as I learned to mother you each how you need, and for continuing to be patient as your needs change and I have to adapt. Thank you for loving my food and being bottomless pits so I never get rusty and often have to get creative when we need to go grocery shopping. I love you, I love you, I love you, I love you. Before I met you, when we're together, when we're apart, and long after my soul leaves this body, I love you & I've got your backs.

Last but certainly not least, thank YOU. Thank you for trying out my recipes & buying this book - you're helping feed an army, or it feels like I'm cooking for an army, it's mostly my three boys.

One Love,

xx Jessica Klein

INDEX